Ca...
Ph...

2nd Edition

by Samantha Tame
and Sam Neang Seoun

Contents

4 Contents

6 Contents

Introduction

"Negotiate a river by following its bends, enter a country by following its customs." – *Cambodian proverb*

It is very useful to learn some of the Cambodian language if you are visiting Cambodia for business or pleasure. Many Cambodians do not speak much English, especially in less touristy areas, so learning some key phrases in Khmer is essential. The aim of this phrasebook is to allow you to communicate in everyday situations while travelling or spending a while longer in Cambodia, without having to know how to read or write Khmer. Although different accents and dialects exist, the words and phrases in this book will be understood across the vast majority of Cambodia.

This phrasebook is divided into chapters which address the most common situations in which you might need to speak Khmer, including while shopping, eating out or taking transport. The Khmer script for each word and phrase is given so that you can show the book if you are having difficulty making yourself understood.

At the back there is a grammar section which covers the basics of Khmer grammar and sentence formation, for language learners who want to know a little more. Then there is an alphabetical list of additional useful vocabulary which does not fall neatly into any of the chapters.

Each chapter also includes travel tips and cultural notes to help you make the most of your stay.

We have tried to make this book as easy to use as possible for someone new to the Khmer language, and we hope that this phrasebook will be useful during your travels.

Pronunciation

It is difficult to write Khmer pronunciation accurately using the English alphabet because many sounds in Khmer simply do not exist in the English language. Some sounds are hard to pronounce, especially some of the vowel sounds, and will take time and practice to master.

Unlike some other Asian languages such as Chinese and Thai, Khmer is not tonal. Syllables are pronounced clearly and separately, not linked together like they are in English. Word stress falls on the last syllable of a word or phrase. For example, the word for 'guesthouse' is pronounced *phteh som-NAK* with the stress at the end.

Consonants

Unless listed below, consonants in this book are pronounced more or less as in English.

Consonants have their full pronunciation at the beginning or middle of a word but are 'unreleased' at the end of a word. For example, think of how in English, the final consonants of words such as *lab, stop, beat,* and *back* aren't pronounced with the little 'explosion' of air that they would have at the beginning of a word.

ch	between the **ch** in **ch**eese and **j** in **j**am.
chh	as in **ch**eese.
h	as in **h**ave when at the start of a word. It can also be pronounced at the end of a word.
k	hard as in s**k**in.
kh	breathy as in **k**ill.
ñ	as the Spanish **ñ** in ma**ñ**ana.
p	hard as in s**p**in.

ph	breathy as in **p**at.
t	hard as in s**t**uck.
th	breathy as in **t**ap.
r	at the beginning or a middle of a word, r is rolled as in Spanish. At the end of a word it is silent.
v	pronounced softly, close to **w** as in **w**et.

Vowels

Unless listed below, vowel sounds in this book can be read as if in English. Sounds marked with (*) have no equivalent in English.

aa	a long **a** as in c**a**r
ae	like the vowel sound in b**i**ke
aeu*	a-uh (pronounce *a* and then *uh* with no pause)
ai	like **eye** but more exaggerated
ao	as in c**ow**
ea	as in y**eah**
é	a short sound as in caf**é**
ie	as in **ear**
eu	as in b**ir**d
ey*	uh-ee (pronounce *uh* and then *ee* with no pause)
oa	as in g**oa**t
or	as in l**aw**
ov*	a-ew (pronounce *a* and then *ew* with no pause)
ua*	oo-uh (pronounce *oo* and then *uh* with no pause)
ueu*	ew-uh (pronounce *ew* and then *uh* with no pause)
'	a 'break' between two syllables

Top ten phrases

If you're ten minutes from landing in Cambodia and haven't learnt a word of Khmer yet, don't worry! Here are ten key phrases that you can use straight away.

1. Jum reab suar ជំរាបសួរ

A polite way to say "hello".

2. Sok sabai សុខសប្បាយ

Literally, "Safe and happy". Can be used as a question or a statement to mean: "How are you?", " I'm fine" or "Take care".

3. Ort té, or kun អត់ទេអរគុណ

"No, thank you." A polite way to decline offers of tuk-tuks, massage, souvenirs or anything else you may be offered in the street.

4. Som beer muay kaew សុំប៉ៀរមួយកែវ

"A draft beer, please." Self-explanatory.

5. Yoa nih muay យកនេះមួយ

"I'll take one of these." Combine it with pointing to ask for what you want in a shop or restaurant.

6. Nih thlai ponmaan? នេះថ្លៃប៉ុន្មាន ?

Ask for the price of something in a shop or market. "How much is this?" You might not understand the answer just yet, but speaking some Khmer can reduce the price a little.

7. Thlai nah! ថ្លៃណាស់

"Too expensive!", coupled with a good-natured grimace, implies that you are not satisfied with the price and want to bargain.

8. Khñom roa phteh somnak muay ខ្ញុំរកផ្ទះសំណាក់មួយ

"I'm looking for a guesthouse." If you've arrived in town without a reservation, ask around and find a place to stay.

9. Bai chha muay chan បាយឆាមួយចាន

"A plate of fried rice" will get you fed anywhere in Cambodia.

10. Or kun chraeun អរគុណច្រើន

"Thanks very much."

Essentials

A traditional Khmer greeting is the *sampeah*, which involves pressing your palms together in front of your body. When meeting someone of your own age, a *sampeah* at chest level is appropriate. To show more respect to someone older than you, the fingertips should touch the nose. To show the utmost respect to someone very important, the fingertips touch the forehead and the head is bowed. This gesture can be used when saying hello, goodbye, to apologize, or to show gratitude. Urban Cambodians may offer a handshake to Westerners but will be pleased if you know the *sampeah*.

Many words for 'you' exist in Khmer, but foreigners are not expected to know all of them. When starting out, it is fine to use the word 'neak'. This word is polite and can be used with someone you do not know well. See p. 73 when you are ready for more forms of address.

Greetings

Hello	សួស្ដី	suasdey
Hello (formal)	ជំរាបសួរ	jum reab suar
Good morning	អរុណសួស្ដី	arun suasdey
Good afternoon	សាយណ្ហ:សួស្ដី	sayon suasdey
Good night	រាត្រីសួស្ដី	reatrey suasdey
How are you?	សុខសប្បាយទេ ?	sok sabai té?

I'm fine	ខ្ញុំសុខសប្បាយ	khñom sok sabai
I'm not fine	ខ្ញុំមិនស្រួលខ្លួនទេ	khñom min srual khluan té
How about you?	ចុះអ្នកវិញ	choh neak viñ?
Have you eaten already? (a friendly greeting)	ញ៉ាំបាយ ?	nyam bai?
Yes, I've eaten	ញ៉ាំរួចហើយ	nyam ruaj haeuy
Not yet	នៅទេ	nov té
Goodbye	លាហើយ	lia haeuy
Goodbye (formal)	ជំរាបលា	chum reab lia
Good luck	សំណាងល្អ	somnang la'or
See you later	ជួបគ្នាពេលក្រោយ	chuab knia pel krowee

Yes, no and politeness

According to Cambodian etiquette, the feet are considered dirty and so you should remove your shoes when entering a home or temple building.

Women are expected to dress on the conservative side, with shoulders and knees covered, especially when visiting temples and religious sites. At the beach or swimming pool you can wear a swimsuit or bikini, although locals usually swim in their clothes.

While spending time in Cambodia you will certainly notice orange-robed monks pacing the streets in the morning collecting alms. Monks are highly respected in Cambodian culture, so give them space and let them pass in front of you. If you wish to take a photo of a monk while visiting a pagoda, ask their permission first.

Showing anger is considered a loss of face and Cambodians find this embarrassing. It's worth bearing in mind that Cambodians often smile, laugh or act impassively to cover annoyance or embarrassment. If things aren't going your way, try to remain calm and patient, as showing your irritation will not work in your favour.

Yes (male speaker)	បាទ	baat
Yes (female speaker)	ចា៎	cha
No	អត់ទេ	ort té
I don't know	ខ្ញុំមិនដឹងទេ	khñom min dung té
Please	សុំ	som
Thank you	អរគុណ	or kun
Thank you very much	អរគុណច្រើន	or kun chraeun
You're welcome, it's OK	មិនអីទេ	min ey té
I'm sorry	សុំទោស	som toah
Excuse me	សុំអត់ទោស	som ort toah

Introducing yourself

When meeting someone for the first time, it is polite to give a *sampeah* as described above.

Most Cambodians will introduce themselves with their surname before their given name.

Name

What's your name?	តើអ្នកឈ្មោះអ្វី ?	taeu neak chhmuah avey?
My name is...	ខ្ញុំឈ្មោះ ...	khñom chhmuah...
His/her name is...	គាត់ឈ្មោះ ...	koat chhmuah...
Nice to meet you	រីករាយដែលបាន ជួបអ្នក	reek reay dael baan chuab neak

Age

It might seem a bit rude when Cambodians want to know your age as soon as they meet you, but they are usually just deciding how formally to speak to you. (See p. 25 for numbers.)

How old are you?	តើអ្នកអាយុ ប៉ុន្មាន ?	taeu neak ayoo ponmaan?
I'm ... years old.	ខ្ញុំមានអាយុ ... ឆ្នាំ	khñom mien ayoo ... chhnam

Nationality

Cambodians are generally interested in meeting people from other countries and may approach you just to practise their English.

90% of Cambodia's population is ethnic Khmer. Other main ethnic groups include Chinese, Cham and Vietnamese.

Country words in Khmer generally come from the French language. The word *barang* means 'French' but is also used to refer to Western foreigners in general, like the Thai *farang*.

Which country are you from?	តើអ្នកមកពីប្រទេស ណា ?	taeu neak mok pee broteh na?
I'm from...	ខ្ញុំមកពី ...	khñom mok pee...
Australia	ប្រទេសអូស្ត្រាលី	broteh ostralee
Cambodia	ប្រទេសកម្ពុជា	broteh kampuchea
Canada	ប្រទេសកាណាដា	broteh kanada
China	ប្រទេសចិន	broteh chin
England	ប្រទេសអង់គ្លេស	broteh onkleh
France	ប្រទេសបារាំង	broteh barang
Germany	ប្រទេសអាល្លឺម៉ង់	broteh allemong

Italy	ប្រទេសអ៊ីតាលី	broteh italee
Japan	ប្រទេសជប៉ុន	broteh japon
Korea	ប្រទេសកូរ៉េ	broteh koré
New Zealand	នូវែលហ្សេឡង់	nouvel zelong
Spain	ប្រទេសអេស្ប៉ាញ	broteh españ
Thailand	ប្រទេសថៃ	broteh thai
USA	សហរដ្ឋអាមេរិក	saharod aamérik
Vietnam	ប្រទេសវៀតណាម	broteh vietnam

Cambodian towns and provinces

Many urban Cambodians are originally from other provinces and love to talk about where they come from. They may return to their hometown to visit family during Buddhist festivals throughout the year.

There are 24 provinces in Cambodia, plus Phnom Penh which is technically a municipality. The newest province is Tboung Khmum, which was formed in 2014, and was formerly part of Kampong Cham Province.

Each province has a capital city, which in many cases has the same name as the province itself. Each province subdivided into districts (srok), subdistricts (khum), quarters (sangkat) and villages (phum).

Which province are you from?

តើអ្នកមកពីខេត្តណា ?

taeu neak mok pee khet na?

Which town/city are you from?

តើអ្នកមកពីក្រុងណា ?

taeu neak mok pee krong na?

I'm from...

ខ្ញុំមកពី

khñ... ok pee...

Province	Province Capital City
Banteay Meanchey បន្ទាយមានជ័យ	Sisophon សិរីសោភ័ណ
Battambang បាត់ដំបង	Battambang បាត់ដំបង
Kampong Cham កំពង់ចាម	Kampong Cham កំពង់ចាម
Kampong Chhnang កំពង់ឆ្នាំង	Kampong Chhnang កំពង់ឆ្នាំង
Kampong Speu កំពង់ស្ពឺ	Chbar Mon ច្បារមន
Kampong Thom កំពង់ធំ	Stung Saen ស្ទឹងសែន
Kampot កំពត	Kampot កំពត
Kandal កណ្ដាល	Ta Khmau តាខ្មៅ
Koh Kong កោះកុង	Koh Kong កោះកុង
Kep កែប	Kep កែប

Province	**Province Capital City**
Kratié	Kratié
ក្រចេះ	ក្រចេះ
Mondolkiri	Sen Monorom
មណ្ឌលគីរី	សែនមនោរម្យ
Oddar Meanchey	Samraong
ឧត្តរមានជ័យ	សំរោង
Pailin	Pailin
ប៉ៃលិន	ប៉ៃលិន
Phnom Penh	Phnom Penh
ភ្នំពេញ	ភ្នំពេញ
Preah Sihanouk	Preah Sihanouk
ព្រះសីហនុ	ព្រះសីហនុ
Preah Vihear	Tbeng Meanchey
ព្រះវិហារ	ត្បែងមានជ័យ
Pursat	Pursat
ពោធិ៍សាត់	ពោធិ៍សាត់
Prey Veng	Prey Veng
ព្រៃវែង	ព្រៃវែង
Ratanakiri	Banlung
រតនគីរី	បានលុង

Province	Province Capital City
Siem Reap	Siem Reap
សៀមរាប	សៀមរាប
Stung Treng	Stung Treng
ស្ទឹងត្រែង	ស្ទឹងត្រែង
Svay Rieng	Svay Rieng
ស្វាយរៀង	ស្វាយរៀង
Takéo	Doun Kaev
តាកែវ	ដូនកែវ
Tboung Khmum	Suong
ត្បូងឃ្មុំ	សួង

Languages

The modern Khmer language is spoken and understood across most of Cambodia. Other languages spoken include Chinese, Cham, Vietnamese and indigenous tribal languages. Some of the older generation still speak French, as Cambodia was under French rule until it regained its independence in 1953.

Young Cambodians generally learn English, Chinese or French as a second language.

Do you speak English?	តើអ្នកចេះនិយាយ ភាសា អង់គ្លេសទេ ?	taeu neak cheh niyeay pheasa onkleh té?

I don't speak English.	ខ្ញុំមិនចេះនិយាយ ភាសាអង់គ្លេសទេ	khñom min cheh niyeay pheasa onkleh té
I speak a little English.	ខ្ញុំចេះនិយាយភាសា អង់គ្លេសតិចតិច	khñom cheh niyeay pheasa ongkleh tic tic
Do you speak Khmer?	តើអ្នកចេះនិយាយ ភាសាខ្មែរទេ ?	taeu neak cheh niyeay pheasa khmer té?
I speak a little Khmer.	ខ្ញុំចេះនិយាយភាសា ខ្មែរតិចតិច	khñom cheh niyeay pheasa khmer tic tic
I don't understand.	ខ្ញុំមិនយល់ទេ	khñom ot yul té
Please speak slowly.	សូមនិយាយយឺត	soom niyeay yeut
Which language(s) do you speak?	តើអ្នកចេះនិយាយ ភាសាអ្វី ?	taeu neak cheh niyeay pheasa avey?
I speak...	ខ្ញុំចេះនិយាយ ...	khñom cheh niyeay...
English	ភាសាអង់គ្លេស	pheasa onkleh
French	ភាសាបារាំង	pheasa barang
German	ភាសាអាល្លឺម៉ង់	pheasa allemong

Italian	ភាសាអ៊ីតាលី	pheasa italee
Japanese	ភាសាជប៉ុន	pheasa japon
Korean	ភាសាកូរ៉េ	pheasa koré
Spanish	ភាសាអេស្ប៉ាញ	pheasa españ
Thai	ភាសាថៃ	pheasa thai
Vietnamese	ភាសាវៀតណាម	pheasa vietnam

Numbers, prices and shopping

The Cambodian currency is called the *riel,* and the exchange rate is 4,000 to 4,100 riel to one US dollar. The US dollar is used throughout Cambodia alongside the riel.

Coins are not used in Cambodia, only banknotes. Shops may not accept dollar notes that are in less than perfect condition, so take care not to crumple or tear them. Most ATMs in Cambodia dispense US dollars, although some also dispense riel. Smaller vendors and tuk-tuk drivers will not carry much change, so be sure to break large dollar notes at large shops or supermarkets.

It is not possible to buy or exchange riel outside of Cambodia, but you can spend US dollars anywhere and will receive a mix of dollars and riel as change. Credit and debit cards are also accepted in some places.

Prices and numbers

In supermarkets and large shops, prices are usually displayed in dollars, while in local markets they are displayed in riel (if at all). Khmer numerals are often used to display prices in riel and these read from left to right in the same way as our numbers, so for example ៥000 is 5,000.

How much is this?	នេះថ្លៃប៉ុន្មាន ?	nih thlai ponmaan?
dollars	ដុល្លារ	dollar
riel	រៀល	riel

26 Numbers, prices and shopping

Number	Numeral	Pronunciation
0	0	soan
1	໑	muay
2	໒	pee
3	៣	bey
4	៤	buan
5	៥	bram
6	៦	bram muay
7	៧	bram pee (or brampel)
8	៨	bram bey
9	៩	bram buan

10	dop	19	dop bram buan
11	dop muay	20	mophey
12	dop pee	21	mophey muay
13	dop bey	22	mophey pee
14	dop buan	23	mophey bey (etc)
15	dop bram	30	sam sep
16	dop bram muay	31	sam sep muay (etc)
17	dop bram pee	40	sai sep
18	dop bram bey	50	ha sep

60	hok sep	**Ordinals**	
70	chet sep	1st	tee muay
80	paet sep	2nd	tee pee
90	kau sep	3rd	tee bey
100	(muay) roy	4th	tee buan
200	pee roy	5th	tee pram
300	bey roy (etc)	6th	tee pram muay
1,000	poan	7th	tee pram pee
2,000	pee poan (etc)	8th	tee pram bey
10,000	meun	9th	tee pram buan
20,000	pee meun (etc)	10th	tee dop
100,000	saen		
1,000,000	lien		

Shopping and bargaining

Cambodia's local markets can be a great place to grab a bargain, whether you're looking for clothes, souvenirs, food or household items. However, vendors often inflate prices for foreigners. If a price seems too high, put on a big smile, suggest a lower one, and prepare to agree on a price somewhere in the middle.

Do you have...	តើអ្នកមាន...	taeu neak mien...
We have	មាន	mien
We don't have	គ្មានទេ	kmien té
How much is this?	នេះថ្លៃប៉ុន្មាន ?	nih thlai ponmaan?

It's too expensive.	ថ្លៃណាស់	thlai nah
Can you give a discount?	ចុះតម្លៃបានទេ	choh tormlai baan té?
Yes, I can.	បាន	baan
No, I can't.	អត់បានទេ	ot baan té
I'll take it.	យកវា	yoa vear
I'll take one of these.	យកនេះមួយ	yoa nih muay
I don't want to buy it.	ខ្ញុំមិនចង់ទិញវាទេ	khñom min chong tiñ vear té

Technology

adaptor	អាដាប់ផ័រ	adaptor
camera	កាមេរ៉ាថត	camera thort
headphones	កាសស្ដាប់ត្រចៀក	kah stab trochiek
laptop	កុំព្យូទ័រយួរដៃ	computer yuar dai
mp3 player	ម៉ាស៊ីនចាក់ MP3	masin chak mp3
phone	ទូរស័ព្ទ	toorasap
phone charger	សាកទូរស័ព្ទ	sak toorasap

phone top-up card	កាតទូរស័ព្ទ	kart toorasap
sim card	ស៊ីមកាត	sim kart
tablet (iPad)	ថេប្លេត	tablet
torch	ពិល	pil

Baggage

backpack	សាកាដូ	sakado
handbag	កាបូប	kabob
laptop bag	កាបូបឡេបថប់	kabob laptop
suitcase	វ៉ាលី	valee
wallet	កាបូបលុយ	kabob luy

Toiletries and hygiene

conditioner	សាប៊ូបណ្ដូន់សក់	saboo bonton sok
condoms	ស្រោមអនាម័យ	sraom anamey
deodorant (roll on)	ប្រដាប់លុញឈៀក	brodop luñ khliek

deodorant (spray)	ប្រដាប់បាញ់បំបាត់ក្លិន	brodop bañ bombat klin
razor	ឡាម	laam
sanitary towels	សំឡីអនាម័យ	somley anamey
shampoo	សាប៊ូកក់សក់	saboo kok sok
soap/body wash	សាប៊ូដុសខ្លួន	saboo doh khluan
tampons	តាមប៉ុន	tampon
toothbrush	ច្រាស់ដុសធ្មេញ	chrah doh thmén
toothpaste	ថ្នាំដុសធ្មេញ	thnam doh thmén
towel	កន្សែង	kornsaeng

Shopping for clothes

Can I try it on?	ខ្ញុំអាចលវារបានទេ ?	khñom aach lo vear baan té?
Yes, you can.	បាន	baan
The changing room is there.	បន្ទប់ផ្លាស់ខោអាវនៅទីនោះ:	bontub phlah khoa aaw nov tee nuh

No, you can't.	អត់បានទេ	ot baan té
Does it fit?	តើវាល្មមទេ ?	taeu vear l'mom té?
It fits.	វាល្មមខ្ញុំ	vear l'mom khñom
It's too big.	វាធំពេក	vear thom pék
It's too small.	វាតូចពេក	vear touch pék
Do you like it?	តើអ្នកចូលចិត្តវាទេ	taeu neak cholchet vear té?
I like it.	ខ្ញុំចូលចិត្តវា	khñom cholchet vear
I don't like it.	ខ្ញុំមិនចូលចិត្តវាទេ	khñom min cholchet vea té

Clothes and accessories

belt	ខ្សែក្រវ៉ាត់	khsae krovat
bracelet	ខ្សែដៃ	khsae dai
dress	រ៉ូប	roab
earrings	ក្រវិល	krovil
flip-flops	ស្បែកជើងផ្ទាត់	sbaek jeung phtoat

gloves	ស្រោមដៃ	sraom dai
hat	មួក	muak
jacket	អាវធំ	aaw thom
jeans	ខោខូបិយ	khoa khoboy
jewellery	គ្រឿងអលង្ការ	krueung alongkar
long sleeved	ដៃវែង	dai vaeng
necklace	ខ្សែក	khsae kor
pants (trousers)	ខោ	khoa
raincoat	អាវភ្លៀង	aaw phlieng
ring	ចិញ្ចៀន	chiñ chien
shirt	អាវ	aaw
shoes	ស្បែកជើង	sbaek jeung
short sleeved	ដៃខ្លី	dai khley
shorts	ខោខ្លី	khoa khley
skirt	សំពត់	sompot

socks	ស្រោមជើង	sraom jeung
sunglasses	ជ័នតាខ្មៅ	vaenta khmao
T-shirt	អាវយឺត	aaw yeut
trainers (sport shoes)	ស្បែកជើងកីឡា	sbaek jeung kila
underwear	ខោអាវក្នុង	khoa aaw knong
watch	នាឡិកា	nealika

Colours

Do you have different colours?	តើអ្នកមានពណ៌ ផ្សេងទេ ?	taeu neak mien poa phseng té?
Do you have...	តើអ្នកមាន...	taeu neak mien...
Yes, we have	មាន	mien
No, we don't have	អត់មានទេ	ort mien té
Do you like the colour?	តើអ្នកចូលចិត្ត ពណ៌នេះទេ ?	taeu neak cholchet poa nih té?
This is a nice colour.	ពណ៌ស្អាត	poa sa'at

I don't like this colour.	ខ្ញុំអត់ចូលចិត្តពណ៌ នឹងទេ	khñom ort cholchet poa nung té
Which colour do you like?	តើអ្នកចូលចិត្តពណ៌អ្វី?	taeu neak cholchet poa avey?
I like..	ខ្ញុំចូលចិត្ត	khñom cholchet...
black	ខ្មៅ	khmao
blue	ខៀវ	khiev
brown	ត្នោត	tnaot
gold	មាស	meah
green	បៃតង	baitong
grey	ប្រផេះ	bropheh
orange	ទឹកក្រូច	tuk krouch
pink	ផ្កាឈូក	phka chhouk
purple	ស្វាយ	svay
red	ក្រហម	krohom
silver	ប្រាក់	brak

| white | ស | sor |
| yellow | លឿង | lueung |

Food and drink

The traditional Cambodian diet revolves around rice, noodles, soup and fish. Freshwater fish are native to the Mekong, Bassac and Tonle Sap rivers, and can be served steamed, grilled, fried or dried. Seafood such as shrimp and crab are also very popular. As for meat, few animals or parts of animals go uneaten; Cambodians eat everything from beef, pork and chicken to frog, eel and crocodile.

Cambodian food is heavily influenced by Chinese food, and Chinese favourites such as Kuy Teav are widely enjoyed. Cambodian food also shares similarities with Vietnamese and Thai cuisine, but it uses less chilli and more mild and aromatic flavours. The French brought the baguette to Cambodia during colonial times, and it is still popular today served as a sandwich.

Western cuisine is becoming increasingly popular among young urban Cambodians, especially pizza. A popular, if inauthentic, style of pizza is a thick, pillowy base with a hotdog-stuffed crust, doused in tropical sauce and topped with seafood and pineapple.

Here are some popular Cambodian dishes that are widely available:

Amok, a fish curry with coconut cream, served in a banana leaf

Bok l'hong, a spicy salad of shredded papaya, often served with brined crabs

Bai Chha, the Asian staple fried rice

Bai Sach Chrouk, a breakfast favourite consisting of boiled rice and grilled pork, with an optional egg

Borbor, a rice porridge or congee, often garnished with dried fish or liver and served with fried dough sticks

Banh Chao, a dish of Vietnamese origin consisting of a savoury pancake stuffed with minced pork and beansprouts

Kuy Teav, a soup with rice noodles served with various garnishes such as beansprouts, fresh herbs, lime juice and chilli

Lok Lak, a dish of diced beef, fried with spices and served with tomato and onion

Mee Chha, fried noodles with vegetables and meat

Naem Chao, fresh spring rolls consisting of steamed rice paper wrapped around salad and prawns

Ngam Ngov, chicken soup flavoured with pickled limes

Nom Pang, a baguette sandwich that can be filled with meat, pâté, sardines or eggs

Plea Sach Koa, a salad of lime-cured beef flavoured with herbs, crushed peanuts and chilli

Pong Tia Koan, a duck egg containing a partially developed embryo, which is boiled and served in the shell. Not for the squeamish

Prahok, a fermented fish paste that can be served as a dip with vegetables. It is nicknamed 'Cambodian cheese' because of its pungent smell

Samlor Kako, a fragrant soup made with vegetables and fish

At the restaurant

Are you hungry?	តើអ្នកឃ្លានទេ ?	taeu neak khlien té?
I'm hungry	ខ្ញុំឃ្លាន	khñom khlien
I'm not that hungry	ខ្ញុំមិនឃ្លានទេ	khñom min khlien té

Are you thirsty?	តើអ្នកស្រេកទឹកទេ ?	taeu neak srék tuk té?
I'm thirsty	ខ្ញុំស្រេកទឹក	khñom srék tuk
I'm not that thirsty	ខ្ញុំមិនស្រេកទឹកទេ	khñom min srék tuk té
Are you ready to order?	ហើយនៅ ?	haeuy nov?
What would you like to eat?	តើអ្នកចង់ញ៉ាំអ្វី ?	taeu neak chong nyam avey?
What would you like to drink?	តើអ្នកចង់ពិសារទឹកអ្វី ?	taeu neak chong pisar tuk avey?
I'll have...	ខ្ញុំយក...	khñom yoa...
I'm vegetarian	ខ្ញុំអត់ញ៉ាំសាច់	khñom ort nyam sach
I'm allergic to...	ខ្ញុំអត់អាចញ៉ាំ...	khñom ort aach nyam...
Please don't put...	សូមកុំដាក់...	soom kom dak...
Would you like it spicy?	ចង់អោយហឹរទេ ?	chong owee heur té?
Spicy	ហឹរ	heur
A little spicy	ហឹរតិច	heur tic

Not spicy	មិនហឹរ	min heur
Is it good?	តើវាឆ្ងាញ់ទេ ?	taeu vea chhngañ té?
It's delicious	ឆ្ងាញ់	chhngañ
It's not delicious	មិនឆ្ងាញ់	min chhngañ
Where's the bathroom?	បង្គន់នៅឯណា ?	bongkun nov ae na?
It's over there.	នៅទីនោះ	nov tee nuh
It's upstairs.	ខាងលើ	khang leu
It's downstairs.	ខាងក្រោម	khang kraom
It's at the back.	នៅខាងក្រោយ	nov khang krowee
Bill please	សុំគិតលុយ	som kit luy

List of foods

apple	ប៉ោម	paom
banana	ចេក	chék
beef	សាច់គោ	sach koa
black pepper	ម្រេច	mrech

burger	បឺហ្គឺរ	burger
butter	បឺ	beur
cabbage	ស្ពៃក្តោប	spai kdaop
cake	នំ	nom
candy	ស្ករគ្រាប់	skor kroab
carrot	ការ៉ុត	karot
cheese	ឈីស	chhis
chicken	សាច់មាន់	sach moan
chicken egg	ពងមាន់	pong moan
chilli	ម្ទេស	mcheh
chocolate	សូកូឡា	sokola
coconut	ដូង	doong
crocodile	ក្រពើ	kropeu
cucumber	ត្រសក់	trorsok
dessert	បង្អែម	bongaem

dragon fruit	ផ្លែស្រកានាគ	phlae srokaniek
duck	សាច់ទា	sach tia
duck egg	ពងទា	pong tia
durian	ធូរេន	thoorén
eel	អន្ទង់	antong
egg	ពង	pong
fish	ត្រី	trey
fish sauce	ទឹកត្រី	tuk trey
fried	ឆា	chha
frog	កង្កែប	korng kaeb
fruit	ផ្លែឈើ	phlae chheu
garlic	ខ្ទឹមស	khtum sor
ginger	ខ្ញី	khnyey
grilled	អាំង	ang
guava	ត្របែក	trobaek

ice cream	ការ៉ែម	karém
jackfruit	ខ្នុរ	khnor
lemongrass	ស្លឹកគ្រៃ	sluk krae
lettuce	សាឡាត់	salat
lime	ក្រូចឆ្មា	krooch chhma
lychee	គូលែន	koolén
mango	ស្វាយ	sway
meat	សាច់	sach
milk	ទឹកដោះគោ	tuk dorh koa
mushroom	ផ្សិត	phsut
noodles	មី	mee
onions	ខ្ទឹមបារាំង	khtum barang
orange	ក្រូច	krooch
papaya	ផ្លែល្ហុង	phlae lahong
peanuts	សណ្ដែកដី	sontaek dey

pineapple	ម្នាស់	mnoah
pizza	ភីហ្សា	pizza
pork	សាច់ជ្រូក	sach chrook
potato	ដំឡូងបារាំង	domlong barang
prawns	បង្កង	bong kong
rambutan	សាវម៉ាវ	sao mao
rice	បាយ	bay
rice (boiled)	បាយស	bay sor
rice (fried)	បាយឆា	bay chha
rice (uncooked)	អង្ករ	ongkor
salt	អំបិល	ombul
sandwich	នំបុ័ង	nom pang
seafood	អាហារសមុទ្រ	aha somot
shrimp	បង្គា	bongkea
soup	ស៊ុប	soup

soy sauce	ទឹកស៊ីអ៊ីវ	tuk see ew
spider	ពីងពាង	ping peang
spring rolls	ណែម	naem
tamarind	អម្ពិល	ompil
tofu	តៅហ៊ូ	tau hoo
tomato	ប៉េងប៉ោះ	peng poah
tomato sauce	ទឹកប៉េងប៉ោះ	tuk peng poah
turmeric	រមៀត	romiet
vegetables	បន្លែ	bonlae
wheat	ស្រូវសាលី	srow salee
yogurt	ទឹកដោះគោជូរ	tuk dorh koa choor

Asking for something else

Rice dishes are typically eaten with a fork and spoon. Depending on the dish you may also be given chopsticks. Knives are usually not provided with Cambodian food, but you can ask.

It is common for cutlery to be brought to the table in a glass of hot water. You can dry your cutlery off with a paper napkin before eating. A small bin is often provided for each table, so you can dispose of bones, cans and used paper napkins as you eat.

Please can I have...	សុំ ...	som...
Please can I have some more...	សុំ ... ថែម	som ... thaem
Can I have another...	សុំ ... មួយទៀត	som ... muay tiet
ashtray	ចានគោះបារី	chan kuah barey
chopsticks	ចង្កឹះ	chongkeuh
cup	ពែង	péng
fork	សម	sorm
glass	កែវ	kaew
ice	ទឹកកក	tuk kork
knife	កាំបិត	kambut
paper napkin	ក្រដាស់ជូតមាត់	krodah joot moat
plate	ចាន	chan
spoon	ស្លាបព្រា	slab prea

Drinks

It is not recommended to drink the tap water in Cambodia, but you can buy bottled water absolutely everywhere quite cheaply.

Local brands of bottled water are fine to drink and can cost less than a dollar for a litre.

Coffee is widely enjoyed in Cambodia, and chains of chic coffee shops have sprung up in urban areas serving all kinds of sweet and frothy treats. Coffee is produced in the Mondolkiri region of Cambodia, and it has a pleasant chocolatey flavour. Be sure to try it Cambodian-style: brewed strong and over ice with a thick layer of sweet condensed milk.

Tea is also very popular, and green tea is often provided free with meals in restaurants. It can be drunk hot or over ice.

Fresh coconuts, sugar cane juice and fresh fruit shakes are delicious and widely available from roadside vendors.

A number of lagers are brewed in Cambodia; the better-tasting ones are Angkor, Cambodia and Anchor. Some of the less pleasant alternatives are Leo, Gold Crown and Ganzberg (whose slogan is "The more I drink, the better it tastes"). As the price of beer starts at around 50c for a can or draft, you can afford to try a few. Other locally-produced alcohols are ABC Stout, Bruntys cider, palm wine, rice wine, and the interestingly-named Golden Muscle Wine.

If you drink with Cambodians, you will find that they like to refill your glass often and make a great ceremony of saying 'jol muay' (cheers) before every sip. It is polite to make eye contact and touch your arm with your free hand while saying cheers.

What would you like to drink?	តើអ្នកចង់ពិសារ ទឹកអ្វី ?	taeu neak chong pisar tuk avey?
Please can I have a...	សុំ ... មួយ	som ... muay
Please can I have a glass of...	សុំ ... មួយកែវ	som ... muay kaev

Please can I have a bottle of...	សុំ ... មួយដប	som ... muay dorb
Please can I have a can of...	សុំ ... មួយកំប៉ុង	som ... muay kompong
One more ... please	សុំ ... មួយទៀត	som ... muay tiet
Cheers!	ជល់មួយ	jol muay
beer	បៀរ	beer
coconut (fresh)	ដូងស្រស់	doong srorh
coffee (hot)	កាហ្វេក្តៅ	kafé kdao
coffee (iced)	កាហ្វេទឹកកក	kafé tuk kork
Coke	កូកា	coca
fruit juice	ទឹកផ្លែឈើ	tuk phlae chheu
fruit shake	ទឹកផ្លែឈើក្រឡុក	phlae chheu krolok
green tea	តែបៃតង	tae baitorng
ice	ទឹកកក	tuk kork
lime juice	ទឹកក្រូចឆ្មា	tuk krooch chhma
milk	ទឹកដោះគោ	tuk dorh koa

milk (fresh)	ទឹកដោះគោស្រស់	tuk dorh koa srorh
milk (condensed)	ទឹកដោះគោខាប់	tuk dorh koa khab
orange juice	ទឹកក្រូច	tuk krooch
red wine	ស្រាក្រហម	sra krahom
soda water	ទឹកសូដា	tuk soda
sugar cane juice	ទឹកអំពៅ	tuk ompov
tea	តែ	tae
tea (hot)	តែក្ដៅ	tae kdao
tea (iced)	តែទឹកកក	tae tuk kork
water	ទឹក	tuk
white wine	ស្រាស	sra sor
sugar	ស្ករ	skor
without ice	កុំដាក់ទឹកកក	kom dak tuk kork
without milk	កុំដាក់ទឹកដោះគោ	kom dak tuk dorh koa
without sugar	កុំដាក់ស្ករ	kom dak skor

Accommodation

Accommodation for travellers is available in Cambodian cities and towns, with something to suit every budget. For those on a budget, a dorm room in a backpackers' hostel is the cheapest option and costs just a few dollars per night. However, modest guesthouses are inexpensive by Western standards and offer much more in the way of comfort and privacy. If you're willing to pay top dollar, there are also some excellent luxury hotels owned by big foreign chains.

Finding a place to stay

Is there ... near here?	មាន ... នៅជិតទី នេះ ?	mien ... nov chit tee nih?
a hotel	សណ្ឋាគារ	sontakia
a guesthouse	ផ្ទះសំណាក់	phteh somnak
a cheap guesthouse/hostel	ផ្ទះសំណាក់ថោក	phteh somnak thaok

Booking a room

Do you have a reservation?	តើអ្នកមានបានកក់ មុនទេ ?	taeu neak mien baan kok mun té?
I have a reservation.	ខ្ញុំបានកក់បន្ទប់	khñom baan kok bontup

I booked online.	ខ្ញុំកក់បន្ទប់លើវិបសាយ	khñom kok bontup leu website
I booked by phone.	ខ្ញុំកក់តាមទូរស័ព្ទ	khñom kok tam toorasap
I've paid already.	ខ្ញុំបានបង់រួចហើយ	khñom baan bong ruach haeuy
I haven't reserved.	ខ្ញុំមិនទាន់បានកក់	khñom min toan baan kok
Do you have a room for tonight?	តើអ្នកមានបន្ទប់សម្រាប់យប់នេះទេ	taeu neak mien bontup somrab yup nih té?
We have rooms.	មានបន្ទប់	mien bontup
We have no rooms available.	គ្មានបន្ទប់ទេ	kmien bontup té
How many nights do you want to stay?	តើអ្នកស្នាក់នៅប៉ុន្មានយប់ ?	taeu neak snak nov ponman yup?
I want to stay for ... nights.	ខ្ញុំនៅ ... យប់	khñom nov ... yup
How many people is it for?	សម្រាប់មនុស្សប៉ុន្មាននាក់	somrab monooh ponmaan neak?
It's for...	សម្រាប់ ...	somrab...
One person	ម្នាក់	m'neak

Two people	ពីរនាក់	pee neak
Three people	បីនាក់	bey neak
Four people	បួននាក់	buan neak
What type of bed(s) do you need?	តើអ្នកត្រូវការគ្រែ ប្រភេទណា ?	taeu neak trov kar krae brophét na?
a dormitory	ដម	dorm
a single bed	គ្រែតូច	krae tooch
twin beds	គ្រែតូចពីរ	krae tooch pee
a double bed	គ្រែធំ	krae thom
two double beds	គ្រែធំពីរ	krae thom pee
a child's bed	គ្រែរបស់កុមារ	krae roboh komar
Is there breakfast?	តើមានអាហារ ពេលព្រឹកទេ ?	taeu mien ahaa pel pruk té?
Breakfast is included.	មានអាហារពេល ព្រឹកជាមួយ	mien ahaa pel pruk jia muay

Breakfast costs extra.	មិនគិតអាហារពេលព្រឹកជាមួយទេ	min kit ahaa pel pruk jia muay té
We don't serve breakfast.	យើងអត់មានអាហារពេលព្រឹកទេ	yeung ort mien ahaa pel pruk té
Does the room have...	តើបន្ទប់មាន ...	taeu bontup mien...
The room has...	បន្ទប់មាន ...	bontup mien...
The room doesn't have...	បន្ទប់មិនមាន ...	bontup min mien...
Does the hotel have...	តើសណ្ឋាគារមាន ...	taeu sontakia mien...
The hotel has...	សណ្ឋាគារមាន	sontakia mien...
The hotel doesn't have...	សណ្ឋាគារមិនមាន	sontakia min mien...
How much does it cost per night?	មួយយប់ថ្លៃប៉ុន្មាន ?	muay yup thlai ponman?
It costs... dollars per night.	មួយយប់ ... ដុល្លារ	muay yup ... dollar

How would you like to pay?	តើអ្នកចង់បង់ប្រាក់តាមរៀបណា ?	taeu neak chong bong brak taam robieb na?
I want to pay by card.	ខ្ញុំចង់បង់ប្រាក់តាមកាត	khñom chong bong brak taam kaat
I want to pay cash.	ខ្ញុំចង់បង់លុយសុទ្ធ	khñom chong bong luy sot
We don't accept credit cards.	យើងមិនទទួលលុយតាមកាតឥណទានទេ	yeung min totual luy taam kaat enotien té

Checking in

Can I take your name?	ខ្ញុំអាចសុំឈ្មោះបានទេ ?	khñom aach som chhmuah baan té?
My name is...	ខ្ញុំឈ្មោះ...	khñom chhmuah...
Can I take your passport?	ខ្ញុំអាចសុំលិខិតឆ្លងដែនរបស់អ្នកបានទេ ?	khñom aach som likhit chhlong daen roboh neak baan té?
Here it is.	នេះ	nih

Which floor is my room on?	បន្ទប់របស់ខ្ញុំនៅ ជាន់ទីប៉ុន្មាន?	bontup roboh khñom nov joan tee ponmaan?
The room is on the ... floor.	បន្ទប់នៅជាន់ទី...	bontup nov joan tee...
What time is breakfast?	អាហារពេលព្រឹក ម៉ោងប៉ុន្មាន?	ahaa pel pruk maong ponmaan?
Breakfast is at...	អាហារពេលព្រឹក នៅម៉ោង...	ahaa pel pruk nov maong...
What time is check-out?	Check out ម៉ោង ប៉ុន្មាន?	check out maong ponmaan?
Check-out is at...	Check out នៅ ម៉ោង...	check out nov maong...

Hotel problems

There's a problem with my room.	មានបញ្ហានៅក្នុង បន្ទប់របស់ខ្ញុំ	mien pañ ha nov knong bontup roboh khñom
The .... doesn't work.	... មិនដើរ	... min daeur
The ... is broken.	... ខូច	... khoach

The ... isn't clean.	... មិនស្អាត	... min sa'art
The room is noisy.	បន្ទប់មានសម្លេង វិខាន	bontup mien somleng romkhan
The room has a bad smell.	បន្ទប់មានក្លិនស្អុយ	bontup mien klin sa'oy
The room doesn't have...	បន្ទប់មិនមាន ...	bontup min mien...

Hotel requests

Can I leave some bags here?	តើខ្ញុំអាចទុកកវ៉ាន់ មួយចំនួននៅទីនេះ បានទេ ?	khñom aach tok eyvan muay chomnuan nov tee nih baan té?
Can I make a phone call?	តើខ្ញុំអាចធ្វើការ ហៅទូរស័ព្ទបាន ទេ ?	taeu khñom aach thveu kar hao toorasap baan té?
Can I order room service?	តើខ្ញុំអាចកម្មង់ អាហារមកបន្ទប់ បានទេ ?	taeu khñom aach komong ahaa mok bontup baan té?
Can I check out late?	តើខ្ញុំអាចចាកចេញ យឺតបន្តិចបានទេ ?	taeu khñom aach chak chéñ yeut bontich baan té?

Can I book a taxi?	តើខ្ញុំអាចកក់តាក់ស៊ីបានទេ?	taeu khñom aach kok taxi baan té?
Can I book a tour?	តើខ្ញុំអាចកក់ដំណើរកំសាន្តបានទេ?	taeu khñom aach kok domnaeur komsan baan té?
Can you do my laundry?	តើអ្នកអាចធ្វើការបោកគក់ខោអាវរបស់ខ្ញុំបានទេ?	taeu neak aach thveu kar baok kok khoa aaw roboh khñom baan té?

Hotel facilities and items

air conditioner	ម៉ាស៊ីនត្រជាក់	masin trojék
balcony/terrace	រានហាល	rien hal
bar	បារ	bar
bathtub	អាងងូតទឹក	aang ngoot tuk
bedsheet	កម្រាលពូក	komral pook
bicycles for hire	កង់សម្រាប់ជួល	kong somrab jual
blanket	ភួយ	phuay

door	ទ្វារ	tvear
elevator/lift	ជណ្ដើរប្រអប់	jontaeu bro orb
ensuite bathroom	បន្ទប់មានបន្ទប់ទឹក	bontub mien bontub tuk
fan	កង្ហាល់	konghal
fridge	ទូទឹកកក	too tuk kork
hair dryer	ម៉ាស៊ីនផ្លុំសក់	masin phlom sok
hot water	ទឹកក្ដៅ	tuk kdao
kettle	កំសៀវ	komsiev
laundry service	សេវាកម្មបោកអ៊ុត	sévakam baok ot
light/lightbulb	អំពូលភ្លើង	ompool phleung
massage service	សេវាម៉ាស្សា	séva massa
mosquito net	មុង	mong
phone charger	ឆ្នាំងសាកទូរស័ព្ទ	chhnang sak toorasap
pillow	ខ្នើយ	khnaeuy
pillowcase	ស្រោមខ្នើយ	sraom khnaeuy

remote control	តេឡេទូរទស្សន៍	télé tooratoo
restaurant	ភោជនីយដ្ឋាន	phoajaneetarn
room key	កូនសោបន្ទប់	koan sao bontub
room number	លេខបន្ទប់	lék bontub
room service	សេវាកម្មបន្ទប់	séva kam bontub
safe box	ទូសុវត្ថិភាព	too sovatthepheap
sauna	សូណា	soana
sea view	ទេសភាពសមុទ្រ	tesapheap samot
shared bathroom	បន្ទប់ទឹករួម	bontub tuk ruam
shower	ទឹកផ្កាឈូក	tuk phka chhook
sink/washbasin	កន្លែងបើកទឹក	konlaeng baeuk tuk
soap	សាប៊ូ	saboo
stairs	ជណ្តើរ	jontaeu
swimming pool	អាងហែលទឹក	aang hael tuk
tap/faucet	ក្បាលរ៉ូប៊ីណេ	kbal robiné

toilet	បង្គន់	bongkun
toilet paper	ក្រដាសអនាម័យ	krodah anamey
towel	កន្សែង	konsaeng
TV	ទូរទស្សន៍	tooratoo
wifi	វ៉ាយហ្វាយ	wi fi
wifi password	លេខវ៉ាយហ្វាយ	lék wifi
window	បង្អួច	bong'uach

Local transport, places and directions

Cambodian cities, particularly Phnom Penh, are not designed for walking. There is a lack of pavements and pedestrian crossings, and the traffic is relentless, so if you're trying to get from A to B you'll probably want to catch a ride. Luckily, you'll probably be offered one as soon as you step out of your hotel or guesthouse.

The most obvious way of getting around locally is by motorbike-powered rickshaw (tuk-tuk). To find one, just head for a main road and flag one down. A short trip costs from $2 and up. Some bartering is expected, but always agree the price before setting off. Motorcyle taxis (motodops) are also available, and are a bit cheaper than tuk-tuks. Just be aware that they are also less safe; Cambodian roads are dangerous, and drivers can be reckless. By law, drivers and passengers must wear a helmet, so motodop drivers are supposed to carry a spare helmet with them although not all of them do.

Another option in Phnom Penh is to use a taxi-hailing app. Uber has recently launched and offers a hassle-free way to book a taxi from your smartphone. This can work out cheaper than a tuk-tuk and you don't have to bargain, plus you get to ride in the relative comfort of an air-conditioned taxi. Local alternatives to Uber include Grab, Exnet, Itsumo and PassApp.

In Phnom Penh there is also a public bus system that has improved drastically in recent years. A single journey costs a fixed price of just 1,500 riel. If you download the "Stops Near Me" app, you can view maps of all the routes and track buses in real time. The drawback is that the buses stick to the main boulevards, so you might still have to take a motodop or tuk-tuk to finish your journey unless your destination is very close to the bus stop. Also, the buses can be slow-moving due to Phnom Penh's heavy traffic.

Where do you want to go?	តើអ្នកចង់ទៅ ឯណា ?	taeu neak chong tov ae na?
I want to go to...	ខ្ញុំចង់ទៅ ...	khñom chong tov...
Do you know...	ស្គាល់ ...	skwol...
I know it	ស្គាល់	skwol
I don't know it	អត់ស្គាល់ទេ	ot skwol té
Where is it?	នៅឯណា ?	nov ae na?
It's on street number...	នៅផ្លូវលេខ ...	nov phlow lék...
It's near...	នៅជិត ...	nov chit...
It's opposite...	នៅទល់មុខ ...	nov tool muk...
It's next to...	នៅជាប់ ...	nov joab...
It's behind...	នៅពីក្រោយ ...	nov pee krowee
It's in front of...	នៅខាងមុខ ...	nov khang muk...
It's between...	នៅចន្លោះ ...	nov chonloah...

Places

airport	ព្រលានយន្តហោះ	prolean yun hoah
Angkor Wat	អង្គរវត្ត	angkor wat
ATM	អេធីអឹម	ATM
bakery	ហាងនំ	haang nom
bank	ធនាគារ	thoniakia
bookshop	ហាងសៀវភៅ	haang siew pho
boulevard	មហាវិថី	mohavithee
bridge	ស្ពាន	spien
bus station	ស្ថានីយឡានក្រុង	sthanee laan krong
café	ហាងកាហ្វេ	haang kafé
Choeung Ek (Killing Fields)	ជើងឯក	choeung aek
dentist	ពេទ្យធ្មេញ	pét thméñ
gas station	ហ្គារ៉ាសសាំង	garah sang
guesthouse	ផ្ទះសំណាក់	phteh somnak

hairdresser	ហាងកាត់សក់	haang kat sok
highway (national road)	ផ្លូវជាតិ	phlow jiet
hospital	មន្ទីរពេទ្យ	monteepét
hotel	សណ្ឋាគារ	sontakier
Independence Monument	វិមានឯករាជ្យ	vimien aekareach
Internet café	ហាងកាហ្វេអ៊ីនធឺណិត	hang kafé internet
laundry	កន្លែងបោកអ៊ុត	kornlaeng baok ot
library	បណ្ណាល័យ	banalay
market	ផ្សារ	phsar
massage shop	ហាងម៉ាស្សា	haang massa
mountain	ភ្នំ	phnom
museum	សារមន្ទីរ	saramontee
night market	ផ្សាររាត្រី	phsar reatrey
Old Market	ផ្សារចាស់	phsar chah

pharmacy	ឱសថស្ថាន	aosots taan
phone shop	ហាងទូរស័ព្ទ	haang toorasap
restaurant	ភោជនីយដ្ឋាន	phojaneetaan
river	ស្ទឹង	stung
road	ផ្លូវ	phlow
Royal Palace	ព្រះបរមរាជវាំង	preah borom reach veang
school	សាលារៀន	sala rien
shop	ហាង	haang
supermarket	ផ្សារទំនើប	phsar tomneub
Tuol Sleng (Genocide Museum)	ទួលស្លែង	tuol slaeng
university	សាកលវិទ្យាល័យ	sakol vityalay
wat (temple)	វត្ត	wat

Giving directions

In Cambodia, it's quite common for drivers to claim to know where something is, when they have no idea and will drive for miles the wrong way instead of asking for directions. If possible, look up your destination in advance so that you can help your driver to navigate, and have Google Maps ready in case you get lost.

go straight	ទៅត្រង់	tov trong
turn left	បត់ឆ្វេង	bot chhwéng
turn right	បត់ស្តាំ	bot sdam
it's on the left-hand side	នៅខាងឆ្វេងដៃ	nov khang chhwéng dai
it's on the right-hand side	នៅខាងស្តាំដៃ	nov khang sdam dai
cross the bridge	ឆ្លងកាត់ស្ពាន	chlong kat spien
turn at the traffic light	បត់នៅភ្លើងសុប	bot nov phleung stop
a bit further	បន្តិចទៀត	bontich tiet
stop here	ឈប់នៅទីនេះ	chhob nov tee nih
wait a moment	ចាំមួយភ្លែត	cham muay phlét
please wait for me here	សូមរង់ចាំខ្ញុំនៅទីនេះ	soom rong cham khñom nov tee nih

Long-distance transport

Long-distance buses are an inexpensive way to get around Cambodia and many different bus companies exist. Generally, you get what you pay for; the more expensive bus companies have newer buses and offer more comfort.

Most buses are air-conditioned and some of the larger buses have toilets and wi-fi. Long-distance buses often stop at a restaurant mid-journey to give you the chance to stretch your legs and grab a snack, although the prices at these stop-offs can be a little inflated.

The night bus can be tempting as it means you avoid the heat of the day and save the price of a hotel bed, but be careful. Cambodia's roads are poorly-lit and full of potholes, and drivers can be reckless. Accidents and breakdowns are not uncommon. As well as this, thieves target sleeping travellers and there have been incidents of physical assault. Solo and female travellers in particular should avoid the night bus altogether, and travel in the daytime when it is safer.

There is also the option of taking domestic flights within Cambodia, and while more expensive, this is of course much faster than going by bus. A number of airlines including Cambodia Angkor Air, Cambodia Bayon Airlines and Bassaka Air operate flights between Phnom Penh, Siem Reap and Sihanoukville.

Cambodia does not have an extensive train network, as the railway fell into disrepair during the Civil War and has not been properly rebuilt. However, since 2016 there is a passenger service between Phnom Penh and Sihanoukville, which uses refurbished 1960s trains and offers scenic views and a smoother ride than the bus. Additionally there is a newly-completed line connecting Phnom Penh to the airport.

Buying a ticket

Where do you want to go?	តើអ្នកចង់ទៅណា ?	taeu neak chong tov na?
I want to buy a ticket to...	ខ្ញុំចង់ទិញសំបុត្រទៅ...	khñom chong tiñ sombot tov...

Days

Which day do you want to go?	តើអ្នកចង់ទៅថ្ងៃណា ?	taeu neak chong tov thngai na?
today	ថ្ងៃនេះ	thngai nih
tomorrow	ថ្ងៃស្អែក	thngai sa'aek
next week	សប្ដាហ៍ក្រោយ	sabda krawee
Monday	ថ្ងៃចន្ទ	thngai chan
Tuesday	ថ្ងៃអង្គារ	thngai ongkier
Wednesday	ថ្ងៃពុធ	thngai puth
Thursday	ថ្ងៃព្រហស្បតិ៍	thngai prohoh
Friday	ថ្ងៃសុក្រ	thngai sok

Saturday	ថ្ងៃសៅរ៍	thngai sau
Sunday	ថ្ងៃអាទិត្យ	thngai aatit

Times

What time do you want to go?	តើអ្នកចង់ទៅម៉ោងប៉ុន្មាន	taeu neak chong tov maong ponmaan?
I want to go...	ខ្ញុំចង់ទៅ...	khñom chong tov...
in the morning	ពេលព្រឹក	pel pruk
in the afternoon	ពេលរសៀល	pel rosiel
in the evening	ពេលល្ងាច	pel lanyiech
at night	ពេលយប់	pel yob
What time does the bus leave?	ឡានក្រុងចេញម៉ោងប៉ុន្មាន ?	laan krong chéñ maong ponmaan?
The bus leaves...	ឡានក្រុងចេញ...	laan krong chéñ...
What time does the bus arrive?	ឡានក្រុងដល់ម៉ោងប៉ុន្មាន ?	laan krong dol maong ponmaan?
The bus arrives...	ឡានក្រុងដល់	laan krong dol...

at ... o'clock	ម៉ោង ...	maong...
at five past...	ម៉ោង ... 5 នាទី	maong ... bram nietee
at ten past...	ម៉ោង ... 10 នាទី	maong ... dop nietee
at quarter past...	ម៉ោង ... 15 នាទី	maong ... dop bram nietee
at twenty past...	ម៉ោង ... 20 នាទី	maong ... mophey nietee
at twenty-five past...	ម៉ោង ... 25 នាទី	maong ... mophey bram nietee
at half past...	ម៉ោង ... កន្លះ	maong ... kawnlah
at twenty-five to...	ម៉ោង ... ខ្វះ 25 នាទី	maong ... khvah mophey bram nietee
at twenty to...	ម៉ោង ... ខ្វះ 20 នាទី	maong ... khvah mophey nietee
at quarter to...	ម៉ោង ... ខ្វះ 15 នាទី	maong ... khvah dop bram nietee
at ten to...	ម៉ោង ... ខ្វះ 10 នាទី	maong ... khvah dop nietee

at five to...	ម៉ោង ... ខ្វះ ៥ នាទី	maong ... khvah bram nietee
How long does the journey take?	តើការធ្វើដំណើរមានរយៈពេលប៉ុន្មាន ?	taeu kar thveu domnaeur mien royeak pel ponmaan?
It takes about ... hours.	ប្រហែល ... ម៉ោង	brohael ... maong
How far is it?	តើឆ្ងាយប៉ុណ្ណា ?	taeu chhngay ponna?
It's ... kilometres.	ប្រហែល ... គីឡូម៉ែត្រ	brohael ... kilomaet

Bus facilities

Does the bus have...	តើឡានក្រុងមាន...	taeu laan krong mien...
wi-fi	វ៉ាយហ្វាយ	wi fi
air-conditioning	ម៉ាស៊ីនត្រជាក់	maseen trocheak
a toilet	បង្គន់	bonkun
lay-down beds	គ្រែដេក	krae dék
Yes, it has...	មាន	mien

| No, it doesn't have... | គ្មានទេ | kmien té |

Forms of transport

airport	ព្រលានយន្តហោះ	prolean yun hoah
bicycle	កង់	kong
boat	ទូក	took
bus	ឡានក្រុង	laan krong
bus station	ស្ថានីយឡានក្រុង	sthanee laan krong
mini van	ឡានតូច	laan touch
motorbike taxi	ម៉ូតូឌុប	motodop
motorcycle	ម៉ូតូ	moto
night bus	ឡានក្រុងពេលយប់	laan krong pel yop
plane	យន្តហោះ	yun hoah
seat	កៅអី	kau ey
taxi	តាក់ស៊ី	taxi

ticket	សំបុត្រ	sombot
train	រថភ្លើង	rot phleung
tuk tuk	តុកតុក	tuk tuk

Forms of address

There are many different words for 'you' in Khmer, depending on the age, gender and social status of the speakers.

In Khmer, it is usual to address one another as family, whether or not the speakers are related. For example, you can call a lady who serves you at the market 'ming' (auntie) if she is older than you, or a waiter 'bong' (brother) if he is about your age.

In a romantic relationship, the woman usually calls the man 'bong' and he calls her 'oan', even if the woman is older.

Foreigners are not expected to know all of the different forms of address and 'neak' is generally an appropriate choice when speaking to an adult who you don't know well.

This is not an exhaustive list of forms of address in Khmer; other forms exist, but these are some of the most widely used.

	to a male		to a female	
polite, to someone your age or older	អ្នក	neak	អ្នក	neak
familiar, to friends only	ឯង	aeng	ឯង	aeng
to someone young enough to be your child (lit: niece/nephew)	ក្មួយ	kmuay	ក្មួយ	kmuay
to children or your own child (lit: child)	កូន	koan	កូន	koan

	to a male		to a female	
to someone younger than yourself	អូន	oan	អូន	oan
to your romantic partner (darling)	បងសំឡាញ់	bong somlañ	អូនសំឡាញ់	oan somlañ
to someone your own age or a bit older (lit: brother/sister)	បង	bong	បងស្រី	bong (srey)
to someone about the same age as your parents (lit: uncle/auntie)	ពូ	poo	មីង	ming
	មា	mea (more colloquial)	អ៊ី	ee (Chinese descent)
to someone older than your parents	អុំ	om	អុំ	om
to someone about the same age as your grandparents (lit: grandpa/grandma)	តា	taa	យាយ	yiay
to someone about the same age as your grandparents (especially of Chinese descent)	កុង	kong	ម៉ា	ma
to a teacher	លោកគ្រូ	loak kru	អ្នកគ្រូ	nek kru

	to a male		to a female	
to a doctor	លោកគ្រូពេទ្យ	loak kru pét	អ្នកគ្រូពេទ្យ	nek kru pét
to someone in a high official position	លោក	loak	លោកស្រី	loak srey
to a monk/nun	ព្រះអង្គ	preah ong	ដូនជី	doan ji

Months and dates

Months

It's quite common for Cambodians to be named after the month they were born in, and many of the month names are unisex.

As well as using the proper names for the months, you can simply refer to months by number. For example, the proper name for January is '*Makara*' but it can also simply be called '*khae muay*' (month one).

January	ខែមករា	khae makara
February	ខែកុម្ភៈ	khae kompheak
March	ខែមីនា	khae minia
April	ខែមេសា	khae mésa
May	ខែឧសភា	khae osaphia
June	ខែមិថុនា	khae mithona
July	ខែកក្កដា	khae kakada
August	ខែសីហា	khae seyha
September	ខែកញ្ញា	khae kaña

October	ខែតុលា	khae tola
November	ខែវិច្ឆិកា	khae vichheka
December	ខែធ្នូ	khae thnou

Years

To say the year in Khmer, simply read as if it were a number. For example, 1990 is read as "one thousand nine hundred and ninety" - *muay poan bram buan roy kau sep*. See p. 25 for more on numbers.

Which year were you born in?	តើអ្នកកើតឆ្នាំណា ?	taeu neak kaeut chhnam na?
I was born in...	ខ្ញុំកើតឆ្នាំ...	khñom kaeut chhnam...

Birthdays

Many Cambodians who were born in villages do not know their exact date of birth but have an 'honorary' birthday.

When's your birthday?	ថ្ងៃកំណើតរបស់អ្នកពេលណា ?	thngai komnaeut roboh neak pel na?
My birthday is...	ថ្ងៃកំណើតរបស់ខ្ញុំ...	thngai komnaeut roboh khñom...

Holidays and celebrations

There are many public holidays in the Khmer calendar. On public holidays, shops and banks are closed. During major public holidays such as Pchum Ben, big cities are deserted as Cambodians flock back to their provincial hometowns to celebrate with their families.

Chinese New Year is not an official public holiday in Cambodia, but it is widely celebrated as many Cambodians have Chinese descent.

Holiday	Name in Khmer	Notes
International New Year	Choal Chhnam Sakol ចូលឆ្នាំសកល	1 January
Victory over Genocide Day	Tivea Cheychomneah Leu Robob Braley Pooch Sah ទិវាជ័យជំនះលើ របប ប្រល័យពូជសាសន៍	7 January Marks the anniversary of the end of the Khmer Rouge regime in 1979.
Chinese New Year	Bon Choul Chhnam Chin បុណ្យចូលឆ្នាំចិន	Falls in February; the date depends on the lunar cycle. Not an official public holiday, though many Cambodians of Chinese descent will take the day off to celebrate.

Holiday	Name in Khmer	Notes
Meak Bochea	Meak Bochea មាឃបូជា	Falls in February; the date depends on the lunar cycle. A Buddhist festival commemorating a key event in the life of the Buddha.
International Women's Day	Tivea Sit Neary Antorachiet ទិវាសិទ្ធិនារីអន្តរជាតិ	8 March
Khmer New Year	Bon Choul Chhnam Khmer បុណ្យចូលឆ្នាំខ្មែរ	A 3-day holiday to bring in the Cambodian New Year that usually starts on April 13th or 14th.
International Labour Day	Tivea Polokam Antorachiet ទិវាពលកម្មអន្តរជាតិ	1 May
Visak Bochea Day	Bon Visak Bochea បុណ្យវិសាខបូជា	Falls in May; the date depends on the lunar cycle. Commemorates the birth of Gautama Buddha.

Holiday	Name in Khmer	Notes
King's Birthday	Preah Reach Pithi Bon Chamraeun Preah Chon Preah Mohaksat Norodom Sihamoni ព្រះរាជពិធីបុណ្យចំធើន ព្រះជន្មព្រះមហាក្សត្រ នរោត្តមសីហមុនី	13 May Celebrating the birth of King Norodom Sihamoni in 1953.
Royal Ploughing Ceremony	Preah Reach Pithi Bon Chroat Preah Neangkoal ព្រះរាជពិធីបុណ្យច្រត់ ព្រះនង្គ័ល	Falls in May, with the exact date depending on the lunar cycle. Celebrating the start of the planting season.
International Children's Day	Tivea Komar Antorachiet ទិវាកុមារអន្តរជាតិ	1 June
King's Mother's Birthday	Preah Reach Pithi Bon Chamraeun Preah Chon Norodom Monineath Sihanouk ព្រះរាជពិធីបុណ្យចំធើន ព្រះជននរោត្តមមនី នាថសីហានុ	18 June Celebrating the birth of Queen Mother Norodom Monineath in 1936.

Holiday	Name in Khmer	Notes
Pchum Ben	Bon Pchum Ben បុណ្យភ្ជុំបិណ្ឌ	A 3-day holiday that falls in September or October depending on the lunar cycle. An important Buddhist holiday when Cambodians pay their respects to deceased ancestors.
Constitutional Day	Tivea Brokah Rodtha Thomanuň ទិវាប្រកាសរដ្ឋធម្មនុញ្ញ	24 September Celebrates the signing of the constitution in 1993.
King's Father's Commemoration	Bon Khuab Preah Borom Rotanak Kaod បុណ្យខួបព្រះបរមរតនៈកោដ្ឋ	15 October The anniversary of the death of the King-Father Norodom Sihanouk in 2012.
Paris Peace Treaty	Tivea Santhisaña Sontipheap Krong Paris ទិវាសន្ធិសញ្ញាសន្តិភាពក្រុងប៉ារីស	23 October Commemorating the Paris Peace Accords in 1991.

Holiday	Name in Khmer	Notes
King's Coronation	Preah Reach Pithi Krong Reach Sambot Preah Baromneath Norodom Sihamoni ព្រះរាជពិធីគ្រងរាជ សម្បត្តិ ព្រះបរមនាថ នរោត្តមសីហមុនី	29 October Commemorating the coronation of Norodom Sihamoni in 2004.
Water Festival	Bon Om Took បុណ្យអុំទូក	A 3-day holiday that falls in October or November to coincide with the full moon. Marks the changing of the tides in the Tonle Sap and is celebrated with boat races.
Independence Day	Bon Aekreach Chiet បុណ្យឯករាជ្យជាតិ	9 November Marks independence from the French in 1953.
International Human Rights Day	Tivea Bon Sith Monooh Antorachiet ទិវាបុណ្យសិទ្ធមនុស្ស អន្តរជាតិ	10 December

Family

When getting to know you, Cambodians are often interested in finding out about your family. This is a central part of Cambodian culture, and great importance is placed on looking after your relatives, respecting your elders and remembering your ancestors.

Cambodian people usually live in extended-family households, and it is not uncommon for three generations to live under one roof. Young adults tend to stay living with their parents until they get married, and as there are no state pensions or care homes, families look after their own elderly relatives at home.

The traditional role of Cambodian women has been to cook, clean, take care of children and handle family finances. However, times are changing and young Cambodian women are increasingly keen to get an education and have a career before they consider marriage.

Cambodian weddings and funerals are elaborate affairs that can last for several days. Both often take place in front of the family house, blocking the road with marquees and blaring out Buddhist chanting through loudspeakers from the crack of dawn. You'll know which is which by the colour of the clothes; mourners at a funeral wear white, whereas wedding guests wear bright colours.

Don't be surprised if you are invited to a wedding when you have only just met the bride or groom; Cambodians like to have as large and impressive a wedding as possible, and it is a badge of honour to have foreigners attending. Prepare to be amazed at the sheer amount of food that is served and eaten, and the number of empty beer cans that carpet the floor at the end. Be sure to bring a gift of money for the newlyweds. About $20 is expected, more if you know the couple well.

Q&A: Family

How many brothers and sisters do you have?	តើអ្នកមានបងប្អូនប៉ុន្មាននាក់?	taeu neak mien bong ba'oan ponmaan neak?
I have ... older brother(s)	ខ្ញុំមានបងប្រុស ... នាក់	khñom mien bong broh ... neak
I have ... younger brother(s)	ខ្ញុំមានប្អូនប្រុស ... នាក់	khñom mien ba'oan broh ... neak
I have ... older sister(s)	ខ្ញុំមានបងស្រី ... នាក់	khñom mien bong srey ... neak
I have ... younger sister(s)	ខ្ញុំមានប្អូនស្រី ... នាក់	khñom mien ba'oan srey ... neak
I don't have any brothers or sisters	ខ្ញុំគ្មានបងប្អូនទេ	khñom kmien bong ba'oan té
Are you married?	តើអ្នករៀបការហើយនៅ?	taeu neak rieb kar haeuy nov?
I'm married	ខ្ញុំបានរៀបការហើយ	khñom baan rieb kar haeuy
I'm engaged	ខ្ញុំភ្ជាប់ពាក្យហើយ	khñom phchoab piek haeuy

I have a boyfriend/girlfriend	ខ្ញុំមានសង្សារ	khñom mien songsar
I'm single	ខ្ញុំនៅលីវ	khñom nov liw
Do you have children?	តើអ្នកមានកូនទេ ?	taeu neak mien koan té?
I have ... son(s)	ខ្ញុំមានកូនប្រុស.. នាក់	khñom mien koan broh ... neak
I have ... daughter(s)	ខ្ញុំមានកូនស្រី.. នាក់	khñom mien koan srey ... neak
I don't have any children	ខ្ញុំគ្មានកូនទេ	khñom kmien koan té

Family members

husband	ប្ដី	bdey
wife	ប្រពន្ធ	brorpon
boyfriend/girlfriend	សង្សារ	songsar
fiancé	គូដណ្ដឹង	koo dorndung
siblings	បងប្អូន	bong ba'aon
older brother	បងប្រុស	bong broh

older sister	បងស្រី	bong srey
younger brother	ប្អូនប្រុស	ba'oan broh
younger sister	ប្អូនស្រី	ba'oan srey
parents	ឪពុកម្ដាយ	aupuk mday
father	ឪពុក	aupuk
mother	ម្ដាយ	mday
dad	ប៉ា	pa
mum	ម៉ាក់	mak
father-in-law	ឪពុកក្មេក	aupuk kmék
mother-in-law	ម្ដាយក្មេក	mday kmék
child/children	កូនក្មេង	koan kméng
daughter	កូនស្រី	koan srey
son	កូនប្រុស	koan broh
aunt	មីង	ming
uncle	ពូ	poo

grandmother	យាយ	yiay
grandfather	តា	taa
grandchild	ចៅ	chau

Work and study

Tens of thousands of Western expats live and work in Cambodia, enjoying the relaxed lifestyle and low cost of living. In Phnom Penh there is a large English-teaching industry, with several good international schools and private academies, as well as the possibility of private tutoring. Siem Reap is home to social enterprises and NGOs, and attracts volunteers. The coastline of southern Cambodia, including Sihanoukville, Kampot and Kep, makes an attractive destination for retirees.

If you are heading to Cambodia to work, you will need to make sure you have the appropriate visa. A 30-day "E-class" visa costs $35 and can be bought on arrival at the airport or border crossing. Airport officials may ask for proof of your employment, so bring a contract or job offer letter if you have one.

Make sure not to leave it too late to extend your visa, as there is a penalty of $10 per day if you overstay. You can extend your initial visa for one, three, six or twelve months at a time, and your employer will be able to help you with this.

All foreigners who are employed in Cambodia also need a work permit. This consists of a booklet which your employer must fill in and keep at your workplace for the duration of your contract, and a card which you keep. Your employer will help you to organize the work permit once you have arrived in Cambodia, and you will need it when it is time to renew your visa.

Jobs

What do you do? កើអ្នកធ្វើអ្វីគេ ? taeu neak thveu ey ké?

I'm on vacation	ខ្ញុំមកវិស្សមកាល	khñom visamak kal
I'm travelling	ខ្ញុំកំពុងធ្វើដំណើរ	khñom kompong thveu domnaeur
I'm a volunteer	ខ្ញុំកំពុងស្ម័គ្រចិត្ត	khñom kompong smak chet
I'm working	ខ្ញុំកំពុងធ្វើការ	khñom kompong thveu ka
I don't have a job	ខ្ញុំគ្មានការងារទេ	khñom kmien ka gnea té
I'm retired	ខ្ញុំចូលនិវត្តន៍	khñom choal ni vot
I'm a(n)...	ខ្ញុំគឺជា	khñom keu jia...
accountant	គណនេយ្យករ	koné ney kor
architect	ស្ថាបត្យករ	stabataya kor
builder	កម្មករសំណង់	kom kor somnong
businessperson	អ្នកជំនួញ	neak chomnuañ
chef/cook	ចុងភៅ	chong phov
cleaner	អ្នកអនាម័យ	neak anamay
dentist	ពេទ្យធ្មេញ	pét thméñ

designer	អ្នកចនា	neak rachana
doctor	គ្រូពេទ្យ	kroo pét
driver	អ្នកបើកបរ	neak baeuk bor
engineer	វិស្វករ	visvak kor
farmer	កសិករ	kasek kor
garment worker	កម្មករកាត់ដេរ	kamakor kat dé
government official	មន្ត្រីរដ្ឋាភិបាល	montrey rotha phibal
hairdresser	ជាងកាត់សក់	jieng kat sok
maid/housekeeper	អ្នកថែទាំផ្ទះ	neak thae toam pteh
manager	អ្នកគ្រប់គ្រង	neak krob krong
mechanic	ជាងមេកានិច	jieng mékanich
nanny	មេដោះ	mé dorh
nurse	គិលានុបដ្ឋាយិកា	kilea nobbothayika
office worker	បុគ្គលិកការិយាល័យ	bokoluk kariyalay

police officer	មន្ត្រីប៉ូលីស	montrey polis
salesperson	អ្នកលក់	neak luak
student	និស្សិត	nisut
tailor	ជាងកាត់ដេរ	jieng kat dé
teacher	គ្រូបង្រៀន	kroo bongrien
tour guide	មគ្គុទេសក៍ ទេសចរណ៍	mokkoté tésochor
vet	ពេទ្យសត្វ	pét sat
volunteer	អ្នកស្ម័គ្រចិត្ត	neak smak chet
waiter	អ្នករត់តុ	neak rot tok
writer	អ្នកនិពន្ធ	neak nipon

Workplaces

| Where do you work? | តើអ្នកធ្វើការនៅទីណា ? | taeu neak thveu ka nov tee na? |
| I work at... | ខ្ញុំធ្វើការនៅ ... | khñom thveu ka nov... |

bank	ធនាគារ	thoniakia
company	ក្រុមហ៊ុន	kromhon
embassy	ស្ថានទូត	sthan toot
factory	រោងចក្រ	roang chak
hospital	មន្ទីរពេទ្យ	montee pét
hotel	សណ្ឋាគារ	sontakia
market	ផ្សារ	phsar
ministry	ក្រសួង	krosuang
NGO	អង្គការ	ongkar
office	ការិយាល័យ	kariyalay
restaurant	ភោជនីដ្ឋាន	phojaneetan
school	សាលា	sala
shop	ហាង	haang
university	សាកលវិទ្យាល័យ	sakol vityalay

Study

Education in Cambodia suffered a major setback under the Khmer Rouge regime between 1975 and 1979. The Khmer Rouge sought out and executed large numbers of people considered to be intellectuals, including teachers and anyone who could speak a foreign language.

Today there remains a shortage of good teachers as a result of low salaries and poor conditions in schools. Many students from poor families also drop out of school at a young age, as they have to start working to support their families as soon as they are able. Cambodia has one of the poorest literacy rates in Southeast Asia.

Because of the shortage of state school places, Cambodian schoolchildren attend school for half days instead of full days. Some families compensate by sending their children to extra classes for the other half of the day, and also on weekends. Wealthy families can afford to send their children to private international schools.

Many young Cambodians aspire to study abroad in order to gain a better quality of education. The most popular destinations are Thailand, Australia, France and the US.

Where do you study?	តើអ្នករៀននៅឯណា	taeu neak rien nov ae na?
I study at...	ខ្ញុំរៀននៅ...	khñom rien nov...
primary school	បឋមសិក្សា	bothoma siksa
high school	វិទ្យាល័យ	vityalay
university	សាកលវិទ្យាល័យ	sakol vityalay

What are you studying?	តើអ្នកកំពុងរៀនអ្វី ?	taeu neak kompong rien avey?
I'm studying...	ខ្ញុំកំពុងរៀន...	khñom kompong rien...
accounting	គណនេយ្យ	koné ney
architecture	ស្ថាបត្យកម្ម	stabataya kom
biology	ជីវវិទ្យា	jee veak vitya
business	មុខជំនួញ	muk chomnuañ
chemistry	គីមីវិទ្យា	kimi vitya
Chinese	ភាសាចិន	pheasa chin
computer science	វិទ្យាសាស្ត្រកុំព្យូទ័រ	vitya sah komputer
dentistry	ទន្តសាស្ត្រ	ton sah
design	ការរចនា	ka rachana
economics	សេដ្ឋកិច្ច	setha kich
education	ការអប់រំ	kar abrom
English	ភាសាអង់គ្លេស	pheasa onkleh

fashion	ម៉ូដ	moad
French	ភាសាបារាំង	pheasa barang
history	ប្រវត្តិសាស្ត្រ	bravot sah
hospitality/tourism	បដិសណ្ឋារកិច្ច	bade santhar kich
Japanese	ភាសាជប៉ុន	pheasa japon
Khmer	ភាសាខ្មែរ	pheasa khmaer
law	ច្បាប់	chbab
literature	អក្សរសាស្ត្រ	aksor sah
management	ការគ្រប់គ្រង	kar krob krong
marketing	ទីផ្សារ	tee phsar
mathematics	គណិតវិទ្យា	kanet vitya
medicine	វជ្ជសាស្ត្រ	vecha sah
pharmacy	ឱសថសាស្ត្រ	aosoth sah
philosophy	ទស្សនវិជ្ជា	tosona vitya
physics	រូបវិទ្យា	roob vitya

politics	នយោបាយ	noyobay
psychology	ចិត្តវិទ្យា	chit vitya
sociology	សង្គមវិទ្យា	songkom vitya
veterinary medicine	បសុសាស្ត្រ	basok sah

Massage, hair and beauty

You can pamper yourself from head to toe very cheaply in Cambodia. Establishments range from upmarket salons, which cater to foreigners and well-to-do Cambodians, to side-of-the-road shacks where you can have your hair snipped for a dollar.

Khmer massage is typically given clothed and without oil, and uses pressure and stretching to relieve tension in the legs, arms, back and shoulders. It can be quite firm, so be sure to tell the therapist in advance if you have any injuries or areas you don't want massaged.

Massage

back and shoulder massage	ម៉ាស្សាខ្នងនិងស្មា	massa khnong nung sma
body massage	ម៉ាស្សាខ្លួន	massa khluan
foot massage	ម៉ាស្សាជើង	massa jeung
head massage	ម៉ាស្សាក្បាល	massa kbal
oil massage	ម៉ាស្សាប្រេង	massa breng
30 minutes	កន្លះម៉ោង	kornlah maong
one hour	មួយម៉ោង	muay maong
Massage gently	ម៉ាស្សាតិចតិច	massa tich tich

Massage firmly	ម៉ាស្សាធ្ងន់	massa thngun

Beauty

manicure	ធ្វើក្រចកដៃ	thveu krorchok dai
pedicure	ធ្វើក្រចកជើង	thveu krorchok jeung
waxing/hair removal	បករោម	bok roam
eyebrow	រោមចិញ្ចើម	roam cheñ chaeum
underarm	ក្លៀក	kliek
leg	ជើង	jeung
make-up	ផាត់ម៉ាការយ៉	phat makayé

Hair

wash hair/shampoo	កក់សក់	kok sok
haircut	កាត់សក់	kat sok
trim	កាត់បន្តិច	kat bontich
cut it short	កាត់វាឱ្យខ្លី	kat vea owee khley
blow dry	ផ្លុំឱ្យស្ងួត	phlom owee snguat

| straightening | អ៊ុតឱ្យក្រង់ | ot owee trong |
| hair colouring | លាបពណ៌សក់ | lieb poa sok |

At the doctor or pharmacy

Healthcare in Cambodia is basic compared to the rest of Asia, and the state-run hospitals are unlikely to be of an acceptable standard for major surgery. However, you can generally receive adequate treatment for a minor illness or injury. It is advisable to make sure you have good travel insurance in case you need treatment for an accident or emergency, as the international hospitals are quite expensive.

Prescriptions are not necessary to obtain medicines, so if you know what you need, you can simply ask for it in a pharmacy. However, be careful when buying medicines, as counterfeit drugs are common. If you need medical advice, seek a reputable doctor, as pharmacists are not always qualified. Many medications are available, but some specialist medicines can be hard to find so it's safest to bring a supply of any essential prescriptions from home.

Injuries and body parts

My ... hurts.	ខ្ញុំឈឺ...	khñom chheu...
I've broken...	ខ្ញុំបានបាក់...	khñom baan bak ...
I've cut...	ខ្ញុំបានកាត់...	khñom baan kat ...
ankle	កជើង	kor jeung
arm	ដៃ	dai
back	ខ្នង	khnong

chest	ទ្រូង	troong
ear	ត្រចៀក	trochiek
elbow	កែងដៃ	kéng dai
eye	ភ្នែក	phnék
finger	ម្រាមដៃ	mriem dai
foot	ជើង	jeung
hand	ដៃ	dai
head	ក្បាល	kbal
knee	ជង្គង់	jong kong
leg	ជើង	jeung
neck	ក	kor
shoulder	ស្មា	sma
stomach	ពោះ	puah
throat	បំពង់ក	bompong kor
toe	ម្រាមជើង	mriem jeung

tooth/teeth	ធ្មេញ	thméñ
wrist	កដៃ	kor dai

Illnesses and medical conditions

I've got...	ខ្ញុំ...	khñom...
I need medicine for...	ខ្ញុំត្រូវការថ្នាំ សម្រាប់...	khñom trov kar thnam somrab...
I need a vaccination against...	ខ្ញុំត្រូវការថ្នាំវ៉ា កសាំងសម្រាប់...	khñom trov kar thnam vaksang somrab...
allergy	អាឡែហ្សី	allergie
animal bite	ខាំសត្វ	kham saat
asthma	ជំងឺហឺត	jomngeu heut
bleeding	ចេញឈាម	chéñ chhiem
burn	រលាកភ្លើង	roliek phleung
cancer	ជំងឺមហារីក	jomngeu moharik
cold/flu	ផ្តាសាយ	phda say
constipation	ទល់លាមក	tol lia mok

cough	ក្អក	ka'or
diabetes	ទឹកនោមផ្អែម	tuk noam pha'aem
diarrhoea	ជាកចុករាគ	roak chok riek
dizziness	វិលមុខ	veul muk
epilepsy	ជំងឺស្គុន់	jomngeu skon
fever	គ្រុនក្ដៅ	krun kdao
headache	ឈឺក្បាល	chheu kbal
hepatitis	ជំងឺលោកថ្លើម	jomngeu roliek thlaeum
high blood pressure	សម្ពាធឈាមខ្ពស់	sompiet chhiem khpuarh
indigestion	ជំងឺពិបាកំលាយអាហារ	jomngeu pibaak romleay aahaa
infection	ការឆ្លងមេរោគ	kar chhlong mérok
insomnia	ការគេងមិនលក់	kar kéng min luak
itching	រមាស់	romoh

kidney infection	ការឆ្លងមេរោគក្នុងតម្រងនោម	kar chhlong méroak knong tomrong noam
low blood pressure	សម្ពាធឈាមទាប	sompiet chhiem tieb
low blood sugar	ជាតិស្ករក្នុងឈាមទាប	jiet skor knong chhiem tieb
malaria	ជំងឺគ្រុនចាញ់	jomngeu krun chaň
migraine	ជំងឺឈឺក្បាលប្រកាច់	jomngeu chheu kbal brokach
motion sickness	ជំងឺពុលរលក	jomngeu pool rolok
nausea	ចង់ក្អួត	chong ga'uat
pregnant/ pregnancy	មានផ្ទៃពោះ	mien phtai puah
sneezing	កណ្ដាស់	kandah
rabies	ជំងឺឆ្កែឆ្កួត	jomngeu chhkae chhkuat
rash	ជំងឺកណ្ដួលរមាស់	jomngeu korndual romoah
shortness of breath	ជំងឺស្វះដង្ហើម	jomngeu steah donghaeum

sore throat	ឈឺក	chheu kor
stomach ache	ឈឺពោះ	chheu puah
stomach ulcer	ដំបៅក្រពះ	dombao kropeah
sunburn	រលាកកំដៅថ្ងៃ	roliek komdao thngai
tetanus	តេតាណូស	tétanus
tonsillitis	រោគរលាកបំពង់ក	roak roliek bompong kor
toothache	ឈឺធ្មេញ	chheu thméñ
typhoid	គ្រុនពោះវៀន	krun puah vien
urine infection	ការឆ្លងមេរោគទឹកនោម	kar chhlong méroak tuk noam
vomiting	ក្អួត	ka'uat

Medicines and medical supplies

I need...	ខ្ញុំត្រូវការ	khñom trov kar
antibiotics	អង់ទីប៊ីយ៉ូទិក	angteebiotik
antimalarials	ថ្នាំគ្រុនចាញ់	thnam krun chañ

antiseptic	ថ្នាំកំចាត់មេរោគ	thnam komchak méroak
aspirin	អាស្ពីរីន	aspirin
bandages	បង់រុំរបួស	bong rom robuah
condoms	ស្រោមអនាម័យ	sraom anamay
contraceptive pill	ថ្នាំពន្យារកំណើត	thnam ponyear komnaeut
emergency contraception	ថ្នាំពន្យារកំណើតភ្លាមៗ	thnam ponyear komnaeut phliem phliem
hand sanitizer	ជែលលាងសំអាតដៃ	jel lieng somaat dai
insulin	អាំងស៊ុយលីន	angsuleen
medicine	ថ្នាំ	thnam
mosquito spray	សាប្រាយបាញ់មូស	sabray bañ mooh
needles	មូល	mchol
painkillers	ថ្នាំបំបាត់ការឈឺចាប់	thnam bombat kar chheu chab

paracetamol	ប៉ារ៉ាសេតាមុល	paracetamol
plasters	បង់បិទរបួស	bong bit robuah
pregnancy test	ប្រដាប់ពិនិត្យផ្ទៃពោះ	brodab pinit phtai puah
sunscreen	ឡេការពារកម្ដៅថ្ងៃ	lékar pier komtao thngai
tablets	ថ្នាំគ្រាប់	thnam kroab
vaccination	ថ្នាំវ៉ាក់សាំង	thnam vaksang

Staying a bit longer

Many expats choose to make their home in Cambodia, enjoying the laidback pace of life, year-round hot climate and low cost of living. In Cambodia's major cities, you can buy most of the products and groceries that you might be used to, and you can enjoy leisure activities such as going to the gym and participating in sports. Expat-oriented bars offer karaoke and trivia nights, and serve up pub grub for a taste of home.

Accommodation is available to suit all budgets, whether you're looking for a fancy condo with a pool on the roof, a family house, or a studio apartment. The price of renting is generally very affordable compared with elsewhere in Asia. Furnished houses and apartments are usually equipped with air-conditioning, wifi, a refrigerator, a gas stove and sometimes a washing machine. A "Western-style" bathroom means that you will have a sit-down toilet, although the shower may be directly over it.

It is easy to find accommodation in Cambodia. Properties to rent are often advertised using local Facebook groups, or classifieds sites such as Khmer24. Using an agent can be a quick and convenient way to find a place to live, as they can show you a few different properties that suit your requirements, and it's simply a case of choosing the one you like most.

Getting your own place

I want to buy...	ខ្ញុំចង់ទិញ...	khñom chong tiñ
I want to rent...	ខ្ញុំចង់ជួល...	khñom chong jual
house	ផ្ទះ	phteh

apartment	ផ្ទះល្វែង	phteh lvéng
room	បន្ទប់	bontup
villa	វីឡា	villa
condo	ខុនដូ	condo
I need...	ខ្ញុំត្រូវការ...	khñom trov kar...
air-conditioning	ម៉ាស៊ីនត្រជាក់	masin trojeak
balcony	រានហាល	rien hal
bathroom	បន្ទប់ទឹក	bontup tuk
bedroom	បន្ទប់គេង	bontup kéng
ensuite bathroom	បន្ទប់មានបន្ទប់ទឹក	bontup mien bontup tuk
fridge	ទូទឹកកក	too tuk kork
furniture	គ្រឿងសង្ហារិម	kreueng songha rum
garden	សួន	suan
kitchen	ផ្ទះបាយ	phteh bai
swimming pool	អាងហែលទឹក	aang hael tuk

| washing machine | ម៉ាស៊ីនបោកគក់ | masin baok kok |
| wifi | វ៉ាយហ្វាយ | wifi |

Getting a moto

Taking a tuk-tuk everywhere can get expensive, so if you're staying a while you might want to buy your own transport. Used bicycles and motorcycles are bought and sold amongst expats and change hands fairly cheaply. Maintenance doesn't cost much, and most minor problems can be fixed for a few dollars. For major repairs, ask other expats to recommend you a good garage, as unscrupulous mechanics may charge you a lot for "fixing" your moto only for it to somehow break again two days later.

Cambodian police are extra-viligant for foreigners breaking traffic rules, and will issue fines for the slightest infringement. By law, the driver and passenger must wear a helmet, you cannot drive without both wing mirrors, and only police are allowed to have their headlights on in the daytime. You are supposed to be given a ticket (*sombot*) when you pay a fine, but the police don't always bother to write one out. You should ask for the ticket, though, because without one you can be fined again for the same offence a few hundred metres down the road.

Maintenance

| Please change the oil. | សូមដូរប្រេង | soom door breng |
| Please put air in the tyres. | សូមចាក់ខ្យល់ | soom chak kyul |

Please put in ... dollars' worth of gas.	សូមចាក់សាំង ... ដុល្លារ	soom chak sang ... dollar
Please put in ... litres of gas.	សូមចាក់សាំង ... លីត្រ	soom chak sang ... leet
Please wash my car.	សូមលាងឡាន	soom lieng laan
Please wash my motorbike.	សូមលាងម៉ូតូ	soom lieng moto

Repairs

I have a puncture.	បែកកង់	baek kong
I lost the key.	បាត់សោរ	bat sao
The battery is flat.	អស់អាគុយ	orh aatoy
The brakes don't work.	ប្រាងអត់ស៊ី	brang ort see
The engine is noisy.	ម៉ាស៊ីនលឺសំលេងខ្លាំង	masin leu somleng khlang
The engine is overheating.	ម៉ាស៊ីនក្តៅខ្លាំង	masin kdao khlang
The engine is weak.	ម៉ាស៊ីនខ្សោយ	masin khsowee

The engine won't start.	ម៉ាស៊ីនអត់ឆេះ	masin ort chheh
The headlight doesn't work.	អំពូលមុខអត់ភ្លើ	ompul muk ort phleu
The indicator doesn't work.	ភ្លើងសុីញ៉ាអត់ភ្លើ	phleung sinya ort phleu
The mirror is broken.	កញ្ចក់បែក	kañchok baek
Can you fix it?	តើអ្នកអាចជួស ជុលវាបានទេ ?	taeu neak aach juah jul vea baan té?
How long will it take?	តើចំណាយពេល ប៉ុន្មាន	taeu chomnay pel ponmaan?
How much will it cost?	ថ្លៃប៉ុន្មាន ?	thlai ponmaan?

Flirting and romance

Cambodian culture has a traditional view of marriage. Young people typically get married by the time they are 25, and in most cases the man is a little older than the woman. Marriage is expected to last for life; divorce is unusual. Women are not supposed to have premarital sex, but men are allowed to.

It is acceptable for Cambodians to date or marry foreigners, and it is particularly common to see couples consisting of a Cambodian woman and a Western man, although it certainly happens the other way around too. Under Cambodian law, foreign nationals can marry Cambodian citizens, although the process involves a lot of paperwork and multiple trips to ministries.

The generic words for 'I' and 'you' (*khñom* and *neak*) are given below, but you can adjust them to your situation. In a romantic relationship, the woman calls the man *bong* and he calls her *oan*. These pronouns are also used to refer to the self. So a man can say to a woman '*bong srolañ oan*', to mean 'I love you'.

You're a beautiful woman.	ស្រីស្អាត	srey sa'art
You're a handsome man.	បុរសសង្ហា	boroh songha
Are you single?	តើអ្នកនៅលីវទេ ?	taeu neak nov liw té?
I have a girlfriend/ boyfriend	ខ្ញុំមានសង្សារ ហើយ	khñom mien songsar haeuy
I'm married	ខ្ញុំរៀបការរួចហើយ	khñom rieb kar ruach haeuy
I'm single	ខ្ញុំគឺនៅលីវ	khñom nov liw
Would you like a drink?	តើអ្នកចង់ពិសារ អ្វី ?	taeu neak chong pisar avey?
Can I see you again?	តើខ្ញុំអាចជួបអ្នក ម្ដងទៀតទេ ?	taeu khñom aach juab neak mdong tiet té?
I like you.	ខ្ញុំចូលចិត្តអ្នក	khñom cholchet neak

I really like you.	ខ្ញុំចូលចិត្តអ្នកខ្លាំង ណាស់	khñom cholchet neak khlang nah
I love you.	ខ្ញុំស្រលាញ់អ្នក	khñom srolañ neak
I miss you.	ខ្ញុំនឹកអ្នក	khñom nuk neak
Will you marry me?	តើអ្នកនឹងរៀបការ ជាមួយខ្ញុំទេ ?	taeu neak nung rieb kar jia muay khñom té?
Let's live together.	តស់រស់នៅជាមួយ គ្នា	toh ruah nov jia muay knia
Let's have children together.	តស់យកកូនជា មួយគ្នា	toh yoak koan jia muay knia

Grammar

Spoken Khmer tends to be very flexible about grammar, and speakers often shorten phrases by leaving out pronouns and grammatical words wherever possible. This section details the proper grammatical forms, but bear in mind that the Khmer that you use and hear in the street might sound quite different.

Pronouns

Subject and object pronouns are the same: for example, 'khñom' means both 'I' and 'me'. Pronouns are often omitted in informal speech when the context makes it clear who is being talked about. (See p. 73 for a list of alternative words for "you".)

I, me	ខ្ញុំ	khñom
you	អ្នក	neak
he, she, him, her	គាត់	koat
it	វា	vea
we, us	ពួកយើង	puak yeung (can be shortened to just 'yeung')
they, them	ពួកគេ	puak ké (can be shortened to just 'ké')

Nouns

There are no articles as such in Khmer (i.e. no 'a' or 'the'). It is possible to use the words for 'one' and 'that' to make the meaning clear.

Nouns in Khmer do not have plural forms (i.e. they do not add -s to indicate more than one of something).

| There's a monkey. | មានស្វាមួយ | mien swa muay (lit: have monkey one) |
| The monkey is eating a banana. | ស្វានោះស៊ីចេក | sva nuh see chék (lit: monkey that eat banana) |

To talk about people in general, it is possible to double the noun.

| The organization helps women. | អង្គការជួយស្ត្រីៗ | ongkar juay strey strey |
| Children go to school. | ក្មេងៗទៅសាលារៀន | kméng kméng tov sala rien |

Classifiers

Classifiers are categories that nouns belong to, and are used often in Khmer. In the below two examples, 'bottle' and 'person' are classifiers.

When using classifiers, the word order is noun + number + classifier.

a bottle of water	ទឹកមួយដប	tuk muay dorb (lit: water one bottle)
two girls	ក្មេងស្រីពីរនាក់	kméng srey pee neak (lit: child girl two person)

Here are some of the most common classifiers.

animals and books	ក្បាល	kbal
bottle (of drink etc)	ដប	dorb
glass (of drink etc)	កែវ	kaew
kinds, ways	យ៉ាង	yang
number of times	ដង	dong
pair (of shoes etc)	គូ	koo
people	នាក់	neak
piece, lump, chunk (of ice, earth, wood etc)	ដុំ	dom
plate of food	ចាន	chan

sheets or leaves (of paper, plants etc)	សន្លឹក	sonluk
sticks, branches, guns	ដើម	daeum
sweets, seeds, tablets	គ្រាប់	kroab

Demonstratives

Demonstratives ('this' and 'that') are placed after the noun.

this	នេះ	nih
these	ទាំងនេះ	teng nih
that	នោះ	nuh
those	ទាំងនោះ	teng nuh
this house	ផ្ទះនេះ	pteh nih
that elephant	ដំរីនោះ	domrey nuh
What is this?	តើនេះគឺជាអ្វី ?	taeu nih keu jea avey?

Possession

The word 'roboh' indicates possession.
The word order is object + roboh + person.

of, belonging to	របស់	roboh
my bike	កង់របស់ខ្ញុំ	kong roboh khñom
your house	ផ្ទះរបស់អ្នក	pteh roboh neak

Adjectives

The adjective is placed after the noun it describes.

| a big house | ផ្ទះធំ | pteh thom |

To form the comparative, place *jeang* after the adjective.

| this house is bigger | ផ្ទះនេះធំជាង | pteh nih thom jieng |

To form the superlative, place *jeang ke* after the adjective.

| this house is biggest | ផ្ទះនេះធំជាងគេ | pteh nih thom jieng ke |

For particular emphasis, the adjective can be doubled.

| an extremely big house | ផ្ទះធំៗ | pteh thom thom |

Adverbs

Adverbs are often formed by using *yang*, *jia* or *dowee* before an adjective. Here are some examples.

quickly	យ៉ាងលឿន	yang leuen
mostly	ដោយភាគច្រើន	dowee pheak chraeun
usually	ជាធម្មតា	jia thommada

Verbs: the 'infinitive'

In Khmer, verbs do not conjugate for gender or number. The same form of the verb is used for I, you, he, they, etc.

The sentence order is subject + verb + object, as in English.

Verb tenses are not used strictly. That means that the same form of the verb can be used to talk about past, present or future depending on the context.

I go to the market.	ខ្ញុំទៅផ្សារ	khñom tov phsar
You go to the market.	អ្នកទៅផ្សារ	neak tov phsar
He/she goes to the market.	គាត់ទៅផ្សារ	koat tov phsar

Negation

To make a verb negative, place *ort* or *min* before the verb, and *té* after it.

Kmien is often used in place of *ort mien*.

He doesn't go.	តាត់មិនទៅទេ	koat min tov té
I don't want to go.	ខ្ញុំអត់ចង់ទៅទេ	khñom ot chong tov té
I don't have water.	ខ្ញុំគ្មានទឹកទេ	khñom kmien tuk té

The imperative

Positive commands are the same as the 'infinitive'.

Negative commands use *kom* before the verb.

| Go to school! | ទៅសាលារៀន | tov sala rien |
| Don't worry. | កុំបារម្ភ | kom barom |

The past tense

To form the past tense, put *baan* before the verb.

Baan also has the sense of 'could'.

I went	ខ្ញុំបានទៅ	khñom baan tov
I didn't go/I couldn't go	ខ្ញុំមិនបានទៅទេ	khñom min baan tov té

'Used to', ever and never

The word *thlob* before the verb can mean 'used to' or 'have ever'.

The negative (never) is *min thlob* or *min dael*.

I used to smoke.	ខ្ញុំធ្លាប់ជក់បារី	khñom thlob jok barey
Have you ever been to China?	តើអ្នកធ្លាប់ទៅ ប្រទេសចិនទេ ?	taeu neak thlob tov broteh chin té
I've never smoked.	ខ្ញុំមិនដែលជក់បារី	khñom min dael jok barey
I've never been to China.	ខ្ញុំមិនធ្លាប់ទៅ ប្រទេសចិន	khñom min thlob tov broteh chin

Continuous time

Use 'kompong' before the verb to show an action in progress.

I'm eating	ខ្ញុំកំពុងហូបបាយ	khñom kompong hoab bai

Future time

Use 'nung' before the verb to talk about the future.

I will go for a walk.	ខ្ញុំនឹងដើរលេង	khñom nung daeur léng

Informational (wh-) questions

Questions should begin with the question-marker *taeu*.

Question words (who, what, where...) usually go at the end of the sentence.

how (in what way)	ដោយរបៀបណា	dowee robieb na
how long (duration)	រយៈពេលប៉ុន្មាន	royeak pel ponmaan
how many/how much	ប៉ុន្មាន	ponmaan
how old	អាយុប៉ុន្មាន	ayoo ponmaan
what	អ្វី	avey
what time	ម៉ោងប៉ុន្មាន	maong ponmaan

when	ពេលណា	pel na
where	នៅឯណា	nov ae na
which	ណា	na
who	នរណា	nor na
why	ហេតុអ្វី	hed avey

Yes/no questions

Yes/no questions begin with 'taeu' and end with 'té'.

Can I book a taxi?	តើខ្ញុំអាចកក់ តាក់ស៊ីបានទេ ?	taeu khñom aach kok taxi baan té?

To answer in the affirmative, just repeat the verb.

To answer in the negative, repeat the verb in the negative (i.e. with ot... té or min... té).

Yes, you can	បាន	baan
No, you can't	អត់បានទេ	ot baan té

Index of extra words

This index contains useful words, including common verbs and adjectives, which do not fit into the other sections. These will be useful when you need to form less common phrases which are not given in this book.

but ប៉ុន្តែ pontae

buy ទិញ tiñ

can អាច aach

cat ឆ្មា chhma

cheap ថោក thaok

clean (adjective) ស្អាត sa'at

clean (verb) សម្អាត som'aat

close, closed, shut បិទ but

cold ត្រជាក់ trocheak

come មក mok

come back ត្រឡប់មកវិញ trolob mok viñ

come from មកពី mok pee

come out ចេញមក cheñ mok

confused ច្រឡំ chrolom

cook (verb) ធ្វើម្ហូប thveu mahob

cow គោ koa

crazy ឆ្កួត chhkuat

crocodile ក្រពើ kropeu

dance (verb) រាំ roam

delicious ឆ្ងាញ់ chhngañ

die ស្លាប់ slab

different ខុសគ្នា koh knia

difficult ពិបាក pi bak

dirty កខ្វក់ kakhvak

do ធ្វើ thveu

dog ឆ្កែ chhkae

downstairs ជាន់ក្រោម joan kraom

drink (verb) ពិសារ pisar

drive (a car etc) បើកបរ baeuk bor

easy ស្រួល srual

eat ញ៉ាំ ñam

elephant ដំរី domrey

every គ្រប់ kroab

expensive ថ្លៃ thlai

far ឆ្ងាយ chhngay

fast លឿន leuen

find រកឃើញ rok kheuñ

finish បញ្ចប់ bañchob

fix/repair ជួសជុល juah jool

fly (insect) រុយ ruy

fly (verb) ហើរ haeur

for (in order to) ដើម្បី daeumbey

for (purpose) សម្រាប់ somrab

for (somebody) អោយ owee

forget ភ្លេច phlech

friend មិត្តភក្តិ mit pheak

frog កង្កែប kongkaeb

get married រៀបការ rieb kar

give ផ្តល់ឱ្យ phtal owee

go ទៅ tov

go back (return) ត្រឡប់ទៅវិញ trolob tov viñ

go in, enter ចូល choal

go out, leave ចេញទៅ cheñ tov

good ល្អ la'or

happy រីករាយ reek reay

have មាន mien

hear ឮ lew

help ជួយ juay

hope សង្ឃឹម songkhum

horse សេះ seh

hot ក្តៅ kdao

if ប្រសិនបើ brosun baeu

know (a person or place) ស្គាល់ skwol

know (how to do sth) ចេះ cheh

know (a fact) ដឹង dung

here ទីនេះ tee nih

high ខ្ពស់ khpuarh

important សំខាន់ somkhan

in នៅក្នុង nov knong

intelligent ឆ្លាត chhlaat

last (previous) មុន mun

lazy ខ្ជិល khchul

look មើល meul

learn/study រៀន rien

like ចូលចិត្ត cholchet

lion តោ tao

live រស់ ruah

lizard តុកកែ tok kae

long (length) វែង veng

long (time) យូរ yoor

loud ខ្លាំង khlang

lose បាត់បង់ bat bong

love ស្រលាញ់ srolañ

man ប្រុស boroh

many ច្រើន chraeun

make ធ្វើ thveu

meet ជួប juab

monkey ស្វា svaa

mosquito មូស muh

near នៅជិត nov jit

need (to do sth) ត្រូវ trov

need (a thing) ត្រូវការ trov kar

never មិនដែល min dael

new ថ្មី thmey

next ក្រោយ krowee

not មិន min

now ឥឡូវ ey low

old ចាស់ chah

once ម្ដង mdong

open បើក baeuk

on, over លើ leu

or ឬ rew

other ផ្សេងទៀត phseng tiet

outside ខាងក្រៅ khang krao

person មនុស្សម្នាក់ mnooh mneak

phone ទូរស័ព្ទ toorasap

pig ជ្រូក jrook

play លេង leng

put ដាក់ dak

quiet ស្ងាត់ sngat

rabbit ទន្សាយ tonsay

rain ភ្លៀង phlieng

rat កណ្ដុរ kandor

read អាន aan

real ពិត pit

really មែន men

rent ជួល jual

ride ជិះ jih

run រត់ rot

same ដូចគ្នា doach knia

say ប្រាប់ prab

scared ខ្លាច khlach

scorpion ខ្យាដំរី khya domrey

see ឃើញ kheuñ

sell លក់ luak

send ផ្ញើ phnyaeu

sit អង្គុយ ongkuy

short ខ្លី khley

should គួរតែ kuar tae

shy អៀន ien

sleep គេង keng

slow យឺត yeut

small តូច tooch

smoke (i.e. to smoke cigarettes) ជក់បារី jook barey

snake ពស់ puah

some ខ្លះ khlah

sometimes ពេលខ្លះ pel klah

soon ឆាប់ chhab

speak និយាយ niyeay

spider ពីងពាង ping peang

stand ឈរ chhor

start ចាប់ផ្ដើម chab phdaeum

stay ស្នាក់នៅ snak nov

stop ឈប់ chhob

strong ខ្លាំង khlang

sure ច្បាស់ chbah

swim ហែលទឹក hael tuk

take (an object) យក yoak

take (medicine) លេប leb

tall ខ្ពស់ khpuarh

teach បង្រៀន bongrien

tell ប្រាប់ prab

that (to think that... to say that...) ថា tha

there (at that place) នៅទីនោះ nov tee nuh

there is/there are មាន mien

therefore ដូច្នេះ doachneh

think គិត kit

tiger ខ្លា khla

tired អស់កំលាំង orh komlang

together ជាមួយគ្នា jia muay knia

too (also, as well) ដែរ dae

too (e.g. too much) ពេក pék

translate បកប្រែ bok brae

travel ធ្វើដំណើរ thveu domnaeur

turn on បើក baeuk

turn off បិទ but

under ក្រោម kraom

understand យល់ yul

upstairs ជាន់ខាងលើ joan khang leu

use ប្រើ braeu

usual, normal ធម្មតា thommada

very ណាស់ nah

visit ទៅលេង tov leng

volunteer ស្ម័គ្រចិត្ត smak chet

wait រង់ចាំ rong cham

walk ដើរ daeur

want (to do sth) ចង់ chong

want (a thing) ចង់បាន chong baan

wash លាង lieng

water buffalo ក្របី krobey

weird, strange ចម្លែក chomlek

with ជាមួយ jia muay

woman ស្រី្ត setrey

write សរសេរ sor sé

Notes

Notes

Printed in Great Britain
by Amazon

25221112R00075